Praise for Holloway's Meditative Commentary

"This Meditative Commentary on 1 and 2 Samuel is God-centered. I appreciate how Gary Holloway has opened our hearts to reading this biblical text through the lens of an active God who is dynamically engaged with Israel. This resource facilitates our attentive listening to God's voice in our own circumstances as we meditate on mighty acts of God in Israel. God is the center of this story, and our response must place God at the center. 1 and 2 Samuel provide ample opportunity to encounter God, know our own hearts, and seek wisdom for our present moments."

—**John Mark Hicks,** author of *Meeting God at* The Shack

"At least half of effective, life-changing Bible study is learning to ask good questions: good questions about God, about ourselves, and about what God might be calling us to do through these texts in our contemporary lives and world. Unfortunately, few commentaries move beyond questions of history and critical method, often leaving Bible readers wondering whether Scripture has anything pressing to say to them. This is the niche Holloway's Meditative Commentary fills so admirably. Prepare to be challenged by someone who knows how to ask good questions and how to teach us to ask better ones."

—**Kevin J. Youngblood,** Professor of Biblical Studies, Harding University

1 AND 2 SAMUEL

GOD SPEAKS TO HIS PEOPLE

A MEDITATIVE
COMMENTARY
on the Old Testament

1 AND 2 SAMUEL

GOD SPEAKS TO HIS PEOPLE

GARY HOLLOWAY

LEAFWOOD
PUBLISHERS
an imprint of Abilene Christian University Press

1 AND 2 SAMUEL

God Speaks to His People

LEAFWOOD PUBLISHERS
an imprint of Abilene Christian University Press

ISBN 978-1-68426-436-0 | LCCN 2023049778

Printed in the United States of America

LIBRARY OF CONGRESS CATALOGING-IN-PUBLICATION DATA
Names: Holloway, Gary, 1956- author.
Title: 1 and 2 Samuel : God speaks to his people / Gary Holloway.
Other titles: First and Second Samuel
Description: Abilene, Texas : Leafwood Publishers, [2024] | "A meditative commentary."
Identifiers: LCCN 2023049778 | ISBN 9781684264360 (paperback) | ISBN 9781684268504 (ebook)
Subjects: LCSH: Bible. Samuel—Commentaries.
Classification: LCC BS1325.53 .H65 2024 | DDC 222/.407—dc23/eng/20240320
LC record available at https://lccn.loc.gov/2023049778

Cover design by Bruce Gore
Interior text design by Sandy Armstrong, Strong Design

Leafwood Publishers is an imprint of Abilene Christian University Press.
ACU Box 29138
Abilene, Texas 79699

1-877-816-4455
www.leafwoodpublishers.com

24 25 26 27 28 29 30 / 7 6 5 4 3 2 1

To Melinda Worley

CONTENTS

INTRODUCTION

HEARING GOD IN SCRIPTURE

There are many commentaries, guides, and workbooks on the various books of the Bible. How is this series different? It is not intended to answer all your scholarly questions about the Bible, or even make you an expert in the details of Scripture. Instead, this series is designed to help you hear the voice of God for your everyday life. It is a guide to meditation on the Bible, meditation that will allow the Bible to transform you.

We read in many ways. We might scan the newspaper for information, read a map for location, read a novel for pleasure, or read a textbook to pass a test. These are all good ways to read, depending on our circumstances.

A young soldier far away from home who receives a letter from his wife reads in yet another way. He might scan the letter quickly at first for news and information. But his longing for his beloved causes him to read the letter again and again, hearing her sweet voice in every line. He slowly treasures each word of this precious letter.

Bible Study

So also, there are many good ways to read the Bible, depending on our circumstances. Bible study is absolutely necessary for our life with God. We rightly study the Bible for information. We ask: Who wrote this? When was it written? Who were the original readers? How do these words apply to me? More importantly, we want information about God. Who is he? What does he think of me? What does he want from me?

There is no substitute for this kind of close, dedicated Bible study. We must know what the Bible says to know our standing with God. We therefore read the Bible to discover true doctrine or teaching. But some in their emphasis on the authority and inspiration of the Bible have forgotten that Bible study is not an end in itself. We want to know God through Scripture. We want to have a relationship with the Teacher, not just the teachings.

Jesus tells some of God's people in his day, "You study the Scriptures diligently because you think that in them you have eternal life. These are the very Scriptures that testify about me, yet you refuse to come to me to have life" (John 5:39–40 NIV). He's not telling them to study their Bibles less, but he is reminding them of the deeper purpose of Bible study—to draw us to God through Jesus. Bible study is a means, not an end.

Yet the way many of us have learned to study the Bible may actually get in the way of hearing God. "Bible study" may sound a lot like schoolwork, and many of us were happy to get out of school. "Bible study" may call to mind pictures of intellectuals surrounded by books in Greek and Hebrew, pondering meanings too deep for ordinary people. The method of Bible study that has been popular for some time focuses on the strangeness of the Bible. It was written long ago, far away, and in languages we cannot read. There is a huge gap between us and the original readers of the Bible, a gap that can only be bridged by scholars, not by average folk.

There is some truth and some value in that "scholarly" method. It is true that the Bible was not written originally to us. Knowing ancient languages and customs can at times help us understand the Bible better. However, one unintended result of this approach is to make the Bible distant from the people of God. We may come to think that we can only hear God indirectly through Scripture, that his Word must be filtered through scholars. We may even think that deep Bible study is a matter of mastering obscure information about the Bible.

Meditation

But we read the Bible for more than information. By studying it, we experience transformation, the mysterious process of God at work in us. Through his loving words, God is calling us to life with him. He is forming us into the image of his Son.

Reading the Bible is not like reading other books. We are not simply trying to learn information or master material. Instead, we want to stand under the authority of Scripture and let God master us. While we read the Bible, it reads us, opening the depths of our being to the overpowering love of God. "For the word of God is alive and active. Sharper than any double-edged sword, it penetrates even to dividing soul and spirit, joints and marrow; it judges the thoughts and attitudes of the heart. Nothing in all creation is hidden from God's sight. Everything is uncovered and laid bare before the eyes of him to whom we must give account" (Heb. 4:12–13 NIV).

Opening our hearts to the word of God is meditation. Although this way of reading the Bible may be new to some, it has a long heritage among God's people. The psalmist joyously meditates on the words of God (Ps. 1:2; 39:3; 119:15, 23, 27, 48, 78, 97, 99, 148). Meditation is taking the words of Scripture to heart and letting them ask questions of us. It is slowing down, chewing over a text, listening closely, reading God's message of love to us over and over. This is not a simple, easy, or naïve reading of Scripture, but a process that takes time, dedication, and practice on our part.

There are many ways to meditate on the Bible. One is praying the Scriptures. Prayer and Bible study cannot be separated. One way of praying the Bible is to make the words of a text your prayer. Obviously, the prayer texts of Scripture, especially the Psalms, lend themselves to this. "The LORD is my shepherd" has been the prayer of many hearts.

However, it is proper and helpful to turn the words of the Bible into prayers. Commands from God can become prayers. "You shall have no other gods before me" (Exod. 20:3 NIV) can be prayed, "Lord, keep me from anything that takes your place in my heart." Stories can be prayed. Jesus heals a man born blind (John 9), and so we pray, "Lord Jesus, open my eyes to who you truly are." Even the promises of the Bible become prayers. "Never will I leave you; never will I forsake you" (Heb. 13:5 NIV; see Deut. 31:6) becomes "God, help me know your promise that you are always with me so I may live my life without fear."

Obviously, there are many helpful ways of hearing the voice of God in Scripture. Again, the purpose of Bible reading and study is not to know more about the Bible, much less to pride ourselves as experts on Scripture; instead, we read to hear the voice of our Beloved—we listen for a word of God for us.

Holy Reading

This commentary reflects one ancient way of meditation and praying the Scriptures known as *lectio divina*, or holy reading. This method assumes that God wants to speak to us directly in the Bible, that the passage we are reading is God's Word to us right now. The writers of the New Testament read the Old Testament with this same conviction. They saw the words of the Bible speaking directly to their own situations. They read with humility and with prayer.

The first step along this way of holy reading is listening to the Bible. Choose a biblical text that is not too long. It is helpful to hear Scripture in various translations. The passages in this commentary alternate among the New International Version, the New Living Translation, and the English Standard Version. *Note that this book will not look at every verse in 1 and 2 Samuel.* You may not find a meditation here on your favorite verse. The purpose is to hear God's voice in your current situation, not to cover material or prepare lessons. Get into a comfortable position and maintain silence before God for several minutes. This prepares the heart to listen. Read slowly. Savor each word. Perhaps read aloud. Listen for a particular phrase that speaks to you. Ask God, What are you trying to tell me today?

The next step is to meditate on that phrase. That meditation may include slowly repeating the phrase that seems to be for you today. As you think deeply on it, you might even memorize it. Committing biblical passages to memory allows us to hold them in our hearts all day long. If you keep a journal, you might write the passage there. Let those words sink deeply into your heart.

Then pray those words back to God in your heart. Those words may call up visual images, smells, sounds, and feelings. Pay attention to what God is giving you in those words. Then respond in faith to what those words say to your heart. What do they call you to be and to do? Our humble response might take the form of praise, thanksgiving, joy, confession, or even cries of pain.

The final step in this "holy reading" is contemplation of God. The words from God that we receive deeply in our hearts lead us to him. Through these words, we experience union with the all-powerful God of love. Again, one should not separate Bible reading from prayer. The words of God in Scripture transport us into the very presence of God where we joyfully rest in his love.

What keeps reading the Bible this way from becoming merely our own desires read back into Scripture? How do we know it is God's voice we hear and not our own?

Two things. One is prayer. We are asking God to open our hearts, minds, and lives to him. We ask to hear his voice, not ours and not the voice of the world around us.

The second thing that keeps this from being an exercise in self-deception is to study the Bible in community. By praying over Scripture in a group, we hear God's Word together. God speaks through the other members of our group. The wisdom he gives them keeps us from private, selfish, and unusual interpretations. They help us keep our own voices in check, as we desire to listen to God alone.

How to Use This Commentary

This commentary assists us in holy reading of the Bible. It gives structure to daily personal devotions, family meditation, small group Bible studies, and church classes.

Daily Devotional

Listening, meditation, prayer, contemplation. How does this commentary fit into this way of Bible study? Consider it as a conversation partner. We have taken a section of Scripture and then broken it down into four or five short daily readings. After listening, meditating, praying, and contemplating the passage for the day, use the questions suggested in the commentary to provoke deeper reflection. This provides a structure for a daily fifteen-minute devotional on those days of the week. On the fifth day, read the fifth section or the entire passage, meditate, and then use the questions to reflect on the meaning of the whole scripture. On day six, explore a series of meditations on the passage, which you can treat like conversation with another who has prayed over the text.

If you want to begin daily Bible reading but need guidance, this provides a Monday through Saturday experience that prepares the heart for worship and praise on Sunday. This structure also results in a communal reading of Scripture, instead of a private reading. Even if you use this commentary alone, you are not reading privately. God is at work in you and in the conversation you have with another (the author of the commentary) who has sought to hear God through this passage of the Bible.

Family Bible Study

This commentary can also provide an arrangement for family Bible study. Many Christian parents want to lead their children in daily study but don't know where to begin or how to structure their time. Using the six-day plan outlined above means the entire family can read, meditate, pray, and reflect on the shorter passages, using the questions provided. On day five, your family can review the entire passage, and then on day six, read the meditations in the commentary to prompt reflection and discussion. God will bless our families beyond our imaginations through the prayerful study of his Word.

Weekly Group Study

This commentary can also structure small group Bible study. Each member of the group should have meditated over the daily readings and questions for the five days preceding the group meeting, using the method outlined above. The day before the group meeting, each member should read and reflect on the meditations in the commentary on that passage. You then can meet once a week to hear God's Word together. In that group meeting, the method of holy reading would look something like this:

Listening

1. Five minutes of silence
2. Slow reading of the biblical passage for that week
3. A minute of silent meditation on the passage
4. Briefly share with the group the word or phrase that struck you

Personal Message

5. A second reading of the same passage
6. A minute of silence
7. Where does this touch your life today?
8. Responses: I hear, I see, etc.

Life Response

9. Brief silence
10. What does God want you to do today in light of this word?

Group Prayer

11. Have each member of the group pray aloud for the person on his or her left, asking God to bless the word he has given them.

The procedure suggested here can be used in churches or in neighborhood Bible studies. Church members would use the daily readings Monday to Friday in their daily devotionals. This commentary intentionally provides no readings on the sixth day so we can spend Saturdays as a time of rest—not rest from Bible study, but a time to let God's Word quietly work its way deep into our hearts. Sunday during Bible school or in-home meetings, the group would meet to experience the weekly readings together, using the group method described above. It might be that the sermon for each Sunday could be on the passage for that week.

Some churches have used this structure to great advantage. In the hallways of those church buildings, the talk is not of the local football team or the weather, but of the shared experience of the Word of God for that week.

And that is the purpose of our personal and communal study—to hear the voice of God, our loving Father, who wants us to love him in return. He deeply desires a personal relationship with us. *Father, Son, and Spirit, make a home inside us* (see John 14:16–17, 23). Our loving God speaks to his children! But we must listen for his voice. That listening is not a matter of gritting our teeth and trying harder to hear. Instead, it is part of our entire life with God. That is what Bible study is all about.

Through daily personal prayer and meditation on God's Word and through a communal reading of Scripture, our most important conversation partner, the Holy Spirit, will do his mysterious and marvelous work. Among other things, the Spirit pours God's love into our hearts (Rom. 5:5), bears witness to our spirits that we are God's children (Rom. 8:16), intercedes for us with God (Rom. 8:26), and enlightens us as to God's will (Eph. 1:17).

So this is an invitation to personal daily Bible study, to praying the Scriptures, to sharing with fellow believers, to hearing the voice of God. God will bless us, our families, our churches, and his world if we take the time to be still, listen, and do his word.

THE SPIRITUALITY OF 1 AND 2 SAMUEL

"In those days the word of the LORD was rare" (1 Sam. 3:1 NIV).

Why? Did the Lord not care about his people? Had he abandoned them? Or was it that he spoke but few took the time to listen?

The first book of Samuel tells the story of those who did and did not listen to God. Hannah pours her heart out to God, begging for a child. She hears God answer her in the birth of a son whom she names Samuel, which means "heard of God." Eli and his sons are priests of God, yet his sons refuse to listen to the Lord and are punished. Eli himself serves the Lord for years but does not recognize the voice of God to Samuel until the third call.

Samuel hears God and obeys him all his life. He obeys him even when the people reject both Samuel and God and ask for a king. Samuel anoints Saul, and the Spirit of God comes upon Saul in power, even making him a prophet. But Saul will not consistently listen to God. Saul's refusal to hear and obey leads to the withdrawal of God's Spirit and to the destruction of Saul and his family.

So God speaks to another—to one after his own heart. David hears the call of God and responds in dramatic fashion. He kills Goliath, frees Israel, and even listens to the compassionate heart of God in refusing to kill Saul, God's anointed, even when Saul repeatedly tries to kill David.

Briefly, this is the story of the books of Samuel. But if we think the heroes of this book are Hannah, Samuel, and David, we miss the point.

The hero of every Bible story is the Lord God. It is God who calls priests, prophets, and kings. It is God who redeems his people. It is God who punishes, who forgives, who delivers. It is his voice, his Word, that rules hearts and lives.

"The word of the LORD was rare in those days." Is it also rare in ours? Has God abandoned us? He sent his Son, Jesus, to live and die for us. He raised him from the dead and brought him back to his right hand. After the ascension of Jesus, has God left us on our own to do the best we can to follow the example of Christ? Or does God still speak today?

This study is written with the conviction that God still speaks today. He speaks through the Bible, his Word. He speaks through the lives of faithful Christian friends. He speaks to us through his Spirit, and we speak to him in prayer, as Hannah did. He speaks in all the circumstances of life.

Listening to God may be a frightening experience, but it is more dangerous to live our lives without hearing him. Are we listening? Can we hear his voice and lead others to hear it? When we pray, do we bring our "to-do list" to God and in essence say, "Listen God, I've got stuff for you to do"? Or, like Samuel, do we say, "Speak LORD, your servant is listening." When we hear the voice of God, are we willing to obey? Or, like Saul, do we listen and follow only when it suits us? Are we, like David, people after God's own heart?

This is an invitation to hear the voice of God in 1 and 2 Samuel. Read it in prayer. Listen to what others around you are hearing. Hear what the Spirit is saying to the churches. Come to this book with a humble heart to hear and to do the Word of the Lord.

MEDITATIONS

I SAMUEL

A GOD WHO HEARS

1:1–2:26 NIV

DAY ONE READING AND QUESTIONS

There was a certain man from Ramathaim, a Zuphite from the hill country of Ephraim, whose name was Elkanah son of Jeroham, the son of Elihu, the son of Tohu, the son of Zuph, an Ephraimite. He had two wives; one was called Hannah and the other Peninnah. Peninnah had children, but Hannah had none.

Year after year this man went up from his town to worship and sacrifice to the LORD Almighty at Shiloh, where Hophni and Phinehas, the two sons of Eli, were priests of the LORD. Whenever the day came for Elkanah to sacrifice, he would give portions of the meat to his wife Peninnah and to all her sons and daughters. But to Hannah he gave a double portion because he loved her, and the LORD had closed her womb. Because the LORD had closed Hannah's womb, her rival kept provoking her in order to irritate her. This went on year after year. Whenever Hannah went up to the house of the LORD, her rival provoked her till she wept and would not eat. Her husband Elkanah would say to her, "Hannah, why are you weeping? Why don't you eat? Why are you downhearted? Don't I mean more to you than ten sons?"

Once when they had finished eating and drinking in Shiloh, Hannah stood up. Now Eli the priest was sitting on his chair by the doorpost of the LORD's house. In her deep anguish Hannah prayed to the LORD, weeping bitterly. And she made a vow, saying, "LORD Almighty, if you will only look on your servant's misery and remember me, and not forget your servant but give her a son, then I will give him to the LORD for all the days of his life, and no razor will ever be used on his head."

As she kept on praying to the LORD, Eli observed her mouth. Hannah was praying in her heart, and her lips were moving but her voice was not heard. Eli thought she was drunk and said to her, "How long are you going to stay drunk? Put away your wine."

"Not so, my lord," Hannah replied, "I am a woman who is deeply troubled. I have not been drinking wine or beer; I was pouring out my soul to the LORD. Do not take your servant for a wicked woman; I have been praying here out of my great anguish and grief."

Eli answered, "Go in peace, and may the God of Israel grant you what you have asked of him."

She said, "May your servant find favor in your eyes." Then she went her way and ate something, and her face was no longer downcast.

Early the next morning they arose and worshiped before the LORD and then went back to their home at Ramah. Elkanah made love to his wife Hannah, and the LORD remembered her. So in the course of time Hannah became pregnant and gave birth to a son. She named him Samuel, saying, "Because I asked the LORD for him."

1. *What do you most want from God? Have you asked? Has God heard? Has he answered? Is it possible he has answered but you have not heard him? What happens when we do not get what we want most?*

2. *Like Eli, have you ever initially misread the actions of a sincere seeker after God?*

3. *What can we do to train ourselves to listen to the hearts of others?*

DAY TWO READING AND QUESTIONS

When her husband Elkanah went up with all his family to offer the annual sacrifice to the Lord and to fulfill his vow, Hannah did not go. She said to her husband, "After the boy is weaned, I will take him and present him before the Lord, and he will live there always."

"Do what seems best to you," her husband Elkanah told her. "Stay here until you have weaned him; only may the Lord make good his word." So the woman stayed at home and nursed her son until she had weaned him.

After he was weaned, she took the boy with her, young as he was, along with a three-year-old bull, an ephah of flour and a skin of wine, and brought him to the house of the Lord at Shiloh. When the bull had been sacrificed, they brought the boy to Eli, and she said to him, "Pardon me, my lord. As surely as you live, I am the woman who stood here beside you praying to the Lord. I prayed for this child, and the Lord has granted me what I asked of him. So now I give him to the Lord. For his whole life he will be given over to the Lord." And he worshiped the Lord there.

1. *When you sing hymns to God, do you pay attention to the words and mean what you say, or do you simply mouth the words thoughtlessly? Are the words of our prayers and hymns vows to God? Does he take our words seriously?*

2. *Do our children really belong to us? Do we truly love them when we try to hang on to them?*

3. *How do we give our children to God today?*

DAY THREE READING AND QUESTIONS

Then Hannah prayed and said:

"My heart rejoices in the LORD;
    in the LORD my horn is lifted high.
My mouth boasts over my enemies,
    for I delight in your deliverance.

"There is no one holy like the LORD;
    there is no one besides you;
    there is no Rock like our God.

"Do not keep talking so proudly
    or let your mouth speak such arrogance,
for the LORD is a God who knows,
    and by him deeds are weighed.

"The bows of the warriors are broken,
    but those who stumbled are armed with strength.
Those who were full hire themselves out for food,
    but those who were hungry are hungry no more.
She who was barren has borne seven children,
    but she who has had many sons pines away.

"The LORD brings death and makes alive;
    he brings down to the grave and raises up.
The LORD sends poverty and wealth;

he humbles and he exalts.
He raises the poor from the dust
and lifts the needy from the ash heap;
he seats them with princes
and has them inherit a throne of honor.

"For the foundations of the earth are the LORD's;
on them he has set the world.
He will guard the feet of his faithful servants,
but the wicked will be silenced in the place of darkness.

"It is not by strength that one prevails;
those who oppose the LORD will be broken.
The Most High will thunder from heaven;
the LORD will judge the ends of the earth.

"He will give strength to his king
and exalt the horn of his anointed."

Then Elkanah went home to Ramah, but the boy ministered before the LORD under Eli the priest.

1. *How do you react when God answers your prayers?*

2. *Have you ever burst into song or written poetry to express your gratitude to God? Shouldn't our gratitude be as heartfelt as our sorrows?*

3. *What areas in our society need reversal? Who needs to be brought down? Who should be exalted? Is God at work in our world? Does he bring this reversal through us? How?*

DAY FOUR READING AND QUESTIONS

Eli's sons were scoundrels; they had no regard for the LORD. Now it was the practice of the priests that, whenever any of the people offered a sacrifice, the priest's servant would come with a three-pronged fork in his hand while the meat was being boiled and would plunge the fork into the pan or kettle or caldron or pot. Whatever the fork brought up the priest would take for himself. This is how they treated all the Israelites who came to Shiloh. But even before the fat was burned, the priest's servant would come and say to the person who was sacrificing, "Give the priest some meat to roast; he won't accept boiled meat from you, but only raw."

If the person said to him, "Let the fat be burned first, and then take whatever you want," the servant would answer, "No, hand it over now; if you don't, I'll take it by force."

This sin of the young men was very great in the LORD's sight, for they were treating the LORD's offering with contempt.

But Samuel was ministering before the LORD—a boy wearing a linen ephod. Each year his mother made him a little robe and took it to him when she went up with her husband to offer the annual sacrifice. Eli would bless Elkanah and his wife, saying, "May the LORD give you children by this woman to take the place of the one she prayed for and gave to the LORD." Then they would go home. And the LORD was gracious to Hannah; she gave birth to three sons and two daughters. Meanwhile, the boy Samuel grew up in the presence of the LORD.

Now Eli, who was very old, heard about everything his sons were doing to all Israel and how they slept with the women who served at the entrance to the tent of meeting. So he said to them, "Why do you do such things? I hear from all the people about these wicked deeds of yours. No, my sons; the report I hear spreading among the LORD's people is not good. If one person sins against another, God may mediate for the offender; but if anyone sins against the LORD, who will intercede for them?" His sons, however, did not listen to their father's rebuke, for it was the LORD's will to put them to death.

And the boy Samuel continued to grow in stature and in favor with the LORD and with people.

1. *Why are there so many scandals involving priests and ministers? Do we hold them to a higher standard? Should we? Does God?*

2. *How can we raise our children to be servants of God?*

3. *Can each of our houses become a house of the Lord where our children minister? What are some concrete steps we can take to make them that way?*

DAY FIVE READING AND QUESTIONS

Go back and read 1 Samuel 1:1–2:26.

1. *How willing are we to be honest before God? Do we openly pour out our hearts to him, as Hannah did? Or do we deny our feelings and deepest desires, saying, "I shouldn't feel like this"? Doesn't God want to hear our heartfelt wishes?*

2. *If we can be honest with God, can't we be honest with each other? Which is harder?*

3. *As God's people, are we comfortable with the way things are in our culture and economy? Or do we burn with God's passion for justice? If God exalts the poor and hungry, what can we do to help him in that work?*

Meditation on 1 Samuel 1:1–2:26

Samuel begins not with God speaking but with a woman speaking to God. Our life with God should be like any other healthy relationship—we listen, and we speak from the heart. God answers Hannah with his word made flesh; he gives her a son she names Samuel, "heard of God." She responds to God's gracious response with a prayer of praise. God responds to our cries from the heart with the Word made flesh. We are called to hear him and to respond in praise.

Having given her very heart to the Lord in the person of her son, Hannah lifts her voice in prayer and praise to God. The theme of her song is the power and sovereignty of a God who reverses human fortune. God is her horn (1 Sam. 2:1, a symbol of strength) and will raise up a king, the anointed one, who will be a horn.

Hannah serves a God who breaks the weapons of the violent while strengthening their weak victims. He causes the full to hunger and feeds the empty. He raises the poor, guards the saints, gives children to the barren, and brings life to the dying.

This great reversal is also a central theme in the New Testament. Mary, the mother of Jesus, sings a similar song of hope and deliverance (Luke 1:46–55). Jesus himself often gives examples of this reversal, where the first are last and the last are first. God has a heart for those who suffer oppression and poverty. His Word to them is one of hope and anticipation. Things will not always be the same. God will act. The days of injustice are over. The kingdom of God has come.

What does all this have to do with the birth of one small boy in the hill country of Ephraim? Everything. For God speaks and acts through his chosen ones, his anointed ones. It is God's strength, wisdom, and justice that will fill Samuel. It is God who is the hero of Hannah's story and of ours.

"God who hears, listen to the cries of our hearts. Bring justice to the oppressed. Use your great power to make things right."

A GOD WHO SPEAKS

2:27–4:18; 5:1–4; 5:6–6:6; 6:10, 13–16; 7:1–2 NLT

DAY ONE READING AND QUESTIONS

One day a man of God came to Eli and gave him this message from the LORD: "I revealed myself to your ancestors when they were Pharaoh's slaves in Egypt. I chose your ancestor Aaron from among all the tribes of Israel to be my priest, to offer sacrifices on my altar, to burn incense, and to wear the priestly vest as he served me. And I assigned the sacrificial offerings to you priests. So why do you scorn my sacrifices and offerings? Why do you give your sons more honor than you give me—for you and they have become fat from the best offerings of my people Israel!

"Therefore, the LORD, the God of Israel, says: I promised that your branch of the tribe of Levi would always be my priests. But I will honor those who honor me, and I will despise those who think lightly of me. The time is coming when I will put an end to your family, so it will no longer serve as my priests. All the members of your family will die before their time. None will reach old age. You will watch with envy as I pour out prosperity on the people of Israel. But no members of your family will ever live out their days. The few not cut off from serving at my altar will survive, but only so their eyes can go blind and their hearts break, and their children will die a violent death. And to prove that what I have said will come true, I will cause your two sons, Hophni and Phinehas, to die on the same day!

"Then I will raise up a faithful priest who will serve me and do what I desire. I will establish his family, and they will be priests to my anointed kings forever. Then all of your surviving family will bow before him, begging for money and food. 'Please,' they will say, 'give us jobs among the priests so we will have enough to eat.'"

1. *If all God's promises are dependent on our faith, do we earn our salvation? Are there unconditional promises of God?*

2. *Has your faith ever been damaged by unholy and hypocritical church leaders? Do we sometimes put too much faith in our leaders? Should we trust them more or trust them less?*

3. *Do we want the Lord to judge corrupt leaders? Should we want that?*

DAY TWO READING AND QUESTIONS

Meanwhile, the boy Samuel served the LORD by assisting Eli. Now in those days messages from the LORD were very rare, and visions were quite uncommon.

One night Eli, who was almost blind by now, had gone to bed. The lamp of God had not yet gone out, and Samuel was sleeping in the Tabernacle near the Ark of God. Suddenly the LORD called out, "Samuel!"

"Yes?" Samuel replied. "What is it?" He got up and ran to Eli. "Here I am. Did you call me?"

"I didn't call you," Eli replied. "Go back to bed." So he did.

Then the LORD called out again, "Samuel!"

Again Samuel got up and went to Eli. "Here I am. Did you call me?"

"I didn't call you, my son," Eli said. "Go back to bed."

Samuel did not yet know the LORD because he had never had a message from the LORD before. So the LORD called a third time, and once more Samuel got up and went to Eli. "Here I am. Did you call me?"

Then Eli realized it was the LORD who was calling the boy. So he said to Samuel, "Go and lie down again, and if someone calls again, say, 'Speak, LORD, your servant is listening.'" So Samuel went back to bed.

And the LORD came and called as before, "Samuel! Samuel!"

And Samuel replied, "Speak, your servant is listening."

Then the LORD said to Samuel, "I am about to do a shocking thing in Israel. I am going to carry out all my threats against Eli and his family, from beginning to end. I have warned him that judgment is coming upon his family forever, because his sons are blaspheming God and he hasn't disciplined them. So I have vowed that the sins of Eli and his sons will never be forgiven by sacrifices or offerings."

Samuel stayed in bed until morning, then got up and opened the doors of the Tabernacle as usual. He was afraid to tell Eli what the LORD had said to him. But Eli called out to him, "Samuel, my son."

"Here I am," Samuel replied.

"What did the LORD say to you? Tell me everything. And may God strike you and even kill you if you hide anything from me!" So Samuel told Eli everything; he didn't hold anything back. "It is the LORD's will," Eli replied. "Let him do what he thinks best."

As Samuel grew up, the LORD was with him, and everything Samuel said proved to be reliable. And all Israel, from Dan in the north to Beersheba in the south, knew that Samuel was confirmed as a prophet of the LORD. The LORD continued to appear at Shiloh and gave messages to Samuel there at the

Tabernacle. And Samuel's words went out to all the people of Israel.

1. *Does God still speak today? How? What can we do to hear him more clearly?*

2. *Is it easier to hear good news from God than it is to hear words of judgment?*

3. *How can we train ourselves to accept bad news from God? Does God still judge us?*

DAY THREE READING AND QUESTIONS

At that time Israel was at war with the Philistines. The Israelite army was camped near Ebenezer, and the Philistines were at Aphek. The Philistines attacked and defeated the army of Israel, killing 4,000 men. After the battle was over, the troops retreated to their camp, and the elders of Israel asked, "Why did the LORD allow us to be defeated by the Philistines?" Then they said, "Let's bring the Ark of the Covenant of the LORD from Shiloh. If we carry it into battle with us, it will save us from our enemies."

So they sent men to Shiloh to bring the Ark of the Covenant of the LORD of Heaven's Armies, who is enthroned between the cherubim. Hophni and Phinehas, the sons of Eli, were also there with the Ark of the Covenant of God. When all the Israelites saw the Ark of the Covenant of the LORD coming into the camp, their shout of joy was so loud it made the ground shake!

"What's going on?" the Philistines asked. "What's all the shouting about in the Hebrew camp?" When they were told it was because the Ark of the LORD had arrived, they panicked. "The gods have come into their camp!" they cried. "This is a disaster! We have never had to face anything like this before! Help! Who can save us from these mighty gods of Israel? They are the same gods who destroyed the Egyptians with plagues when Israel was in the wilderness. Fight as never before, Philistines! If you don't, we will become the Hebrews' slaves just as they have been ours! Stand up like men and fight!"

So the Philistines fought desperately, and Israel was defeated again. The slaughter was great; 30,000 Israelite soldiers died that day. The survivors turned and fled to their tents. The Ark of God was captured, and Hophni and Phinehas, the two sons of Eli, were killed.

A man from the tribe of Benjamin ran from the battlefield and arrived at Shiloh later that same day. He had torn his clothes and put dust on his head to show his grief. Eli was waiting beside the road to hear the news of the battle, for his heart trembled for the safety of the Ark of God. When the messenger arrived and told what had happened, an outcry resounded throughout the town.

"What is all the noise about?" Eli asked.

The messenger rushed over to Eli, who was ninety-eight years old and blind. He said to Eli, "I have just come from the battlefield—I was there this very day."

"What happened, my son?" Eli demanded.

"Israel has been defeated by the Philistines," the messenger replied. "The people have been slaughtered, and your two sons, Hophni and Phinehas, were also killed. And the Ark of God has been captured."

When the messenger mentioned what had happened to the Ark of God, Eli fell backward from his seat beside the gate. He broke his neck and died, for he was old and overweight. He had been Israel's judge for forty years.

1. *Doesn't God judge us individually for our sin? Does he still punish others for our sins? Do others—family, church, nation, planet—suffer because we disobey?*

2. *Is there a connection between this passage and the idea of "disciplining" wayward church members?*

3. *Why does Israel bring the ark into battle? Is this an attempt to manipulate God? Do we ever put God in a box and think we can control him? What does God think of those efforts?*

DAY FOUR READING AND QUESTIONS

After the Philistines captured the Ark of God, they took it from the battleground at Ebenezer to the town of Ashdod. They carried the Ark of God into the temple of Dagon and placed it beside an idol of Dagon. But when the citizens of Ashdod went to see it the next morning, Dagon had fallen with his face to the ground in front of the Ark of the LORD! So they took Dagon and put him in his place again. But the next morning the same thing happened—Dagon had fallen face down before the Ark of the LORD again. This time his head and hands had broken off and were lying in the doorway. Only the trunk of his body was left intact. . . .

Then the LORD's heavy hand struck the people of Ashdod and the nearby villages with a plague of tumors. When the people realized what was happening, they cried out, "We can't keep the Ark of the God of Israel here any longer! He is against us! We will all be destroyed along with Dagon, our god." So they called together the rulers of the Philistine towns and asked, "What should we do with the Ark of the God of Israel?"

The rulers discussed it and replied, "Move it to the town of Gath." So they moved the Ark of the God of Israel to Gath. But when the Ark arrived at Gath, the LORD's heavy hand fell on its men, young and old; he struck them with a plague of tumors, and there was a great panic.

So they sent the Ark of God to the town of Ekron, but when the people of Ekron saw it coming they cried out, "They are bringing the Ark of the God of Israel here to kill us, too!" The people summoned the Philistine rulers again and begged them, "Please send the Ark of the God of Israel back to its own country, or it will kill us all." For the deadly plague from God had already begun, and great fear was sweeping across the town. Those who didn't die were afflicted with tumors; and the cry from the town rose to heaven.

1. *God used the evil act of the Philistines, capturing the ark, to punish his people. Does God use the evil of others to punish people today? Does that excuse those who do evil?*

2. *What about war, terrorism, and disease? Does God himself send evil, or does he use evil for his purposes?*

3. *Was the holiness of the Lord a frightening concept to the Philistines? Is it to us? Should we be frightened of God? What is the fear of the Lord?*

DAY FIVE READING AND QUESTIONS

The Ark of the Lord remained in Philistine territory seven months in all. Then the Philistines called in their priests and diviners and asked them, "What should we do about the Ark of the Lord? Tell us how to return it to its own country."

"Send the Ark of the God of Israel back with a gift," they were told. "Send a guilt offering so the plague will stop. Then, if you are healed, you will know it was his hand that caused the plague."

"What sort of guilt offering should we send?" they asked.

And they were told, "Since the plague has struck both you and your five rulers, make five gold tumors and five gold rats, just like those that have ravaged your land. Make these things to show honor to the God of Israel. Perhaps then he will stop afflicting you, your gods, and your land. Don't be stubborn and rebellious as Pharaoh and the Egyptians were. By the time God was finished with them, they were eager to let Israel go. . . ."

So these instructions were carried out. . . .

The people of Beth-shemesh were harvesting wheat in the valley, and when they saw the Ark, they were overjoyed! The cart came into the field of a man named Joshua and stopped beside a large rock. So the people broke up the wood of the cart for a fire and killed the cows and sacrificed them to the Lord as a burnt offering. Several men of the tribe of Levi lifted the Ark of the Lord and the chest containing the gold rats and gold tumors from the cart and placed them on the large rock. Many sacrifices and burnt offerings were offered to the Lord that day by the people of Beth-shemesh. The five Philistine rulers watched all this and then returned to Ekron that same day. . . .

So the men of Kiriath-jearim came to get the Ark of the Lord. They took it to the hillside home of Abinadab and ordained Eleazar, his son, to be in charge of it. The Ark remained in Kiriath-jearim for a long time—twenty years in all. During that time all Israel mourned because it seemed the Lord had abandoned them.

1. *Both Eli and Samuel are called by God. How does each respond to the call? Does God call us to specific acts of service as he called Samuel? If so, how does that work? How can we hear that call?*

2. *What are some ways you see God acting powerfully in your life? Do you expect God to do something? How can we train ourselves to see and hear God at work?*

3. *Are we comfortable with the God of this section of Scripture—a God who kills in battle, sends tumors, and knocks old men off their chairs? Do we get to choose our view of God, or must it be shaped by all of Scripture? Do we have to like God to love him?*

Meditation on 1 Samuel 2:27–4:18; 5:1–4; 5:6–6:6; 6:10, 13–16; 7:1–2

We often talk and sing of our awesome God, a God of infinite power and love. This God is active in our world and in our lives. Do we truly believe he is in control? In Samuel's day, "the word of the Lord was rare; there were not many visions" (1 Sam. 3:1 NIV). Had God stopped working among his people? Or were they too busy, too "religious," or too self-centered to see his work?

The Lord dramatically calls the boy Samuel in the night, but Samuel does not recognize the voice. Thinking it is Eli who calls, Samuel runs to him three times. Eli, who as priest should have been listening to the voice of God, does not realize it is the Lord until the third call. Finally, Eli instructs Samuel on how to respond to the call of God: "Speak, Lord, for your servant is listening" (1 Sam. 3:9 NIV).

The Lord's message is one of action. He is about to do something in Israel. He is about to judge Eli and his family. The next morning Samuel is reticent to tell Eli what the Lord said, but after Eli asks him in the name of God, Samuel repeats the message. To his credit, Eli responds to the message of his doom with acceptance: "He is the Lord; let him do what is good in his eyes" (1 Sam. 3:18 NIV).

This is just the first of many times the Lord will appear to Samuel the prophet. Samuel learns to listen to God. He proclaims the message of the Lord to his people, even when the news is bad. As a result of his faithful listening, God was with Samuel and "let none of Samuel's words fall to the ground" (1 Sam. 3:19 NIV). When Samuel spoke, the people could depend on his words being from God, not from his own wishes or imagination.

"O God who speaks, give us ears to hear and eyes to see what you are about to do among us today."

A GOD WHO IS FAITHFUL

7:3–12; 8:1–9:3; 9:5–6, 15–21; 10:1–11, 17–24; 10:26–12:7; 12:12–12:25 NIV

DAY ONE READING AND QUESTIONS

So Samuel said to all the Israelites, "If you are returning to the LORD with all your hearts, then rid yourselves of the foreign gods and the Ashtoreths and commit yourselves to the LORD and serve him only, and he will deliver you out of the hand of the Philistines." So the Israelites put away their Baals and Ashtoreths, and served the LORD only.

Then Samuel said, "Assemble all Israel at Mizpah, and I will intercede with the LORD for you." When they had assembled at Mizpah, they drew water and poured it out before the LORD. On that day they fasted and there they confessed, "We have sinned against the LORD." Now Samuel was serving as leader of Israel at Mizpah.

When the Philistines heard that Israel had assembled at Mizpah, the rulers of the Philistines came up to attack them. When the Israelites heard of it, they were afraid because of the Philistines. They said to Samuel, "Do not stop crying out to the LORD our God for us, that he may rescue us from the hand of the Philistines." Then Samuel took a suckling lamb and sacrificed it as a whole burnt offering to the LORD. He cried out to the LORD on Israel's behalf, and the LORD answered him.

While Samuel was sacrificing the burnt offering, the Philistines drew near to engage Israel in battle. But that day the LORD thundered with loud thunder against the Philistines and threw them into such a panic that they were routed before the Israelites. The men of Israel rushed out of Mizpah and pursued the Philistines, slaughtering them along the way to a point below Beth Kar.

Then Samuel took a stone and set it up between Mizpah and Shen. He named it Ebenezer, saying, "Thus far the LORD has helped us."

1. *What gods or idols do we follow today? Do we think we can serve them and God also? Do we and our churches need to repent and turn to God?*

2. *Do we trust God to help us when we are surrounded by enemies? What do you fear?*

3. *What are our greatest worries? Can we raise our Ebenezer and believe the Lord will help us?*

DAY TWO READING AND QUESTIONS

When Samuel grew old, he appointed his sons as Israel's leaders. The name of his firstborn was Joel and the name of his second was Abijah, and they served at Beersheba. But his sons did not follow his ways. They turned aside after dishonest gain and accepted bribes and perverted justice.

So all the elders of Israel gathered together and came to Samuel at Ramah. They said to him, "You are old, and your sons do not follow your ways; now appoint a king to lead us, such as all the other nations have."

But when they said, "Give us a king to lead us," this displeased Samuel; so he prayed to the LORD. And the LORD told him: "Listen to all that the people are saying to you; it is not you they have rejected, but they have rejected me as their king. As they have done from the day I brought them up out of Egypt until this day, forsaking me and serving other gods, so they are doing to you. Now listen to them; but warn them solemnly and let them know what the king who will reign over them will claim as his rights."

Samuel told all the words of the LORD to the people who were asking him for a king. He said, "This is what the king who will reign over you will claim as his rights: He will take your sons and make them serve with his chariots and horses, and they will run in front of his chariots. Some he will assign to be commanders of thousands and commanders of fifties, and others to plow his ground and reap his harvest, and still others to make weapons of war and equipment for his chariots. He will take your daughters to be perfumers and cooks and bakers. He will take the best of your fields and vineyards and olive groves and give them to his attendants. He will take a tenth of your grain and of your vintage and give it to his officials and attendants. Your male and female servants and the best of your cattle and donkeys he will take for his own use. He will take a tenth of your flocks, and you yourselves will become his slaves. When that day comes, you will cry out for relief from the king you have chosen, but the LORD will not answer you in that day."

But the people refused to listen to Samuel. "No!" they said. "We want a king over us. Then we will be like all the other nations, with a king to lead us and to go out before us and fight our battles."

When Samuel heard all that the people said, he repeated it before the LORD. The LORD answered, "Listen to them and give them a king."

Then Samuel said to the Israelites, "Everyone go back to your own town."

1. *"Be careful what you pray for; you just might get it." Is this wise advice on prayer? Have you ever insisted that God give you something, only later to be glad he did not (or sorry he did)? What does this say about praying that God's will be done?*

2. *Why doesn't God say no to their request for a king? Parents sometimes allow their children to make their own choices, knowing they will bring bad consequences. Is this good parenting? Is that what God was doing to Israel? Does he do it with us?*

3. *Do Samuel's warnings about the power of the king apply to those of us who live in a democracy and choose our leaders? Do we expect our leaders to solve our problems and protect us, or is our trust in God alone?*

DAY THREE READING AND QUESTIONS

There was a Benjamite, a man of standing, whose name was Kish son of Abiel, the son of Zeror, the son of Bekorath, the son of Aphiah of Benjamin. Kish had a son named Saul, as handsome a young man as could be found anywhere in Israel, and he was a head taller than anyone else.

Now the donkeys belonging to Saul's father Kish were lost, and Kish said to his son Saul, "Take one of the servants with you and go and look for the donkeys." . . .

When they reached the district of Zuph, Saul said to the servant who was with him, "Come, let's go back, or my father will stop thinking about the donkeys and start worrying about us."

But the servant replied, "Look, in this town there is a man of God; he is highly respected, and everything he says comes true. Let's go there now. Perhaps he will tell us what way to take." . . .

Now the day before Saul came, the LORD had revealed this to Samuel: "About this time tomorrow I will send you a man from the land of Benjamin. Anoint him ruler over my people Israel; he will deliver them from the hand of the Philistines. I have looked on my people, for their cry has reached me."

When Samuel caught sight of Saul, the LORD said to him, "This is the man I spoke to you about; he will govern my people."

Saul approached Samuel in the gateway and asked, "Would you please tell me where the seer's house is?"

"I am the seer," Samuel replied. "Go up ahead of me to the high place, for today you are to eat with me, and in the morning I will send you on your way and will tell you all that is in your heart. As for the donkeys you lost three days ago, do not worry about them; they have been found. And to whom is all the desire of Israel turned, if not to you and your whole family line?"

Saul answered, "But am I not a Benjamite, from the smallest tribe of Israel, and is not my clan the least of all the clans of the tribe of Benjamin? Why do you say such a thing to me?" . . .

Then Samuel took a flask of olive oil and poured it on Saul's head and kissed him, saying, "Has not the LORD anointed you ruler over his inheritance? When you leave me today, you will meet two men near Rachel's tomb, at Zelzah on the border of Benjamin. They will say to you, 'The donkeys you set out to look for have been found. And now your father has stopped thinking about them and is worried about you. He is asking, "What shall I do about my son?"'

"Then you will go on from there until you reach the great tree of Tabor. Three men going up to worship God at Bethel will meet you there. One will be carrying three young goats, another three loaves of bread, and another a skin of wine. They will greet you and offer you two loaves of bread, which you will accept from them.

"After that you will go to Gibeah of God, where there is a Philistine outpost. As you approach the town, you will meet a procession of prophets coming down from the high place with lyres, timbrels, pipes and harps being played before them, and they will be prophesying. The Spirit of the LORD will come powerfully upon you, and you will prophesy with them; and you will be changed into a different person. Once these signs are fulfilled, do whatever your hand finds to do, for God is with you.

"Go down ahead of me to Gilgal. I will surely come down to you to sacrifice burnt offerings and fellowship offerings, but you must wait seven days until I come to you and tell you what you are to do."

As Saul turned to leave Samuel, God changed Saul's heart, and all these signs were fulfilled that day. When he and his servant arrived at Gibeah, a procession of prophets met him; the Spirit of God came powerfully upon him, and he joined in their prophesying. When all those who had formerly known him saw him prophesying with the prophets, they asked each other, "What is this that has happened to the son of Kish? Is Saul also among the prophets?" . . .

Samuel summoned the people of Israel to the LORD at Mizpah and said to them, "This is what the LORD, the God of Israel, says: 'I brought Israel up out of Egypt, and I delivered you from the power of Egypt and all the kingdoms that oppressed you.' But you have now rejected your God, who saves you out of all your disasters and calamities. And you have said, 'No, appoint a king over us.' So now present yourselves before the Lord by your tribes and clans."

When Samuel had all Israel come forward by tribes, the tribe of Benjamin was taken by lot. Then he brought forward the tribe of Benjamin, clan by clan, and Matri's clan was taken. Finally Saul son of Kish was taken. But when they looked for him, he was not to be found. So they inquired further of the Lord, "Has the man come here yet?"

And the Lord said, "Yes, he has hidden himself among the supplies."

They ran and brought him out, and as he stood among the people he was a head taller than any of the others. Samuel said to all the people, "Do you see the man the Lord has chosen? There is no one like him among all the people."

Then the people shouted, "Long live the king!" . . .

Saul also went to his home in Gibeah, accompanied by valiant men whose hearts God had touched. But some scoundrels said, "How can this fellow save us?" They despised him and brought him no gifts. But Saul kept silent.

1. *Why does Saul hide among the baggage? Is this humility on his part or disobedience to the call of God?*

2. *Do we ever try to hide from responsibilities God has placed on us? Can this spring from a false sense of humility?*

3. *How does the Holy Spirit work in the life of Saul? What does it mean to be a prophet? Is Saul a prophet like Samuel?*

DAY FOUR READING AND QUESTIONS

Nahash the Ammonite went up and besieged Jabesh Gilead. And all the men of Jabesh said to him, "Make a treaty with us, and we will be subject to you."

But Nahash the Ammonite replied, "I will make a treaty with you only on the condition that I gouge out the right eye of every one of you and so bring disgrace on all Israel."

The elders of Jabesh said to him, "Give us seven days so we can send messengers throughout Israel; if no one comes to rescue us, we will surrender to you."

When the messengers came to Gibeah of Saul and reported these terms to the people, they all wept aloud. Just then Saul was returning from the fields, behind his oxen, and he asked, "What is wrong with everyone? Why are they weeping?" Then they repeated to him what the men of Jabesh had said.

When Saul heard their words, the Spirit of God came powerfully upon him, and he burned with anger. He took a pair of oxen, cut them into pieces, and sent the pieces by messengers throughout Israel, proclaiming, "This is what will be done to the oxen of anyone who does not follow Saul and Samuel." Then the terror of the Lord fell on the people, and they came out together as one. When Saul mustered them at Bezek, the men of Israel numbered three hundred thousand and those of Judah thirty thousand.

They told the messengers who had come, "Say to the men of Jabesh Gilead, 'By the time the sun is hot tomorrow, you will be rescued.'" When the messengers went and reported this to the men of Jabesh, they were elated. They said to the Ammonites, "Tomorrow we will surrender to you, and you can do to us whatever you like."

The next day Saul separated his men into three divisions; during the last watch of the night they broke into the camp of the Ammonites and slaughtered them until the heat of the day. Those who survived were scattered, so that no two of them were left together.

The people then said to Samuel, "Who was it that asked, 'Shall Saul reign over us?' Turn these men over to us so that we may put them to death."

But Saul said, "No one will be put to death today, for this day the LORD has rescued Israel."

Then Samuel said to the people, "Come, let us go to Gilgal and there renew the kingship." So all the people went to Gilgal and made Saul king in the presence of the LORD. There they sacrificed fellowship offerings before the LORD, and Saul and all the Israelites held a great celebration.

1. *Saul basically threatens the Israelites with punishment if they will not heed his call to arms. Is there a place for threats in urging people to do right? Does threat of punishment in hell motivate people? Should it? Or should we always motivate with love?*

2. *The people give Saul credit for the victory, but he credits God. Do we sometimes give too much credit to the "heroes" of the Bible? Do we sometimes take credit for our own victories, instead of praising God?*

3. *Who is in control of our world? Presidents? Voters? Chance? The economy? God?*

DAY FIVE READING AND QUESTIONS

Samuel said to all Israel, "I have listened to everything you said to me and have set a king over you. Now you have a king as your leader. As for me, I am old and gray, and my sons are here with you. I have been your leader from my youth until this day. Here I stand. Testify against me in the presence of the LORD and his anointed. Whose ox have I taken? Whose donkey have I taken? Whom have I cheated? Whom have I oppressed? From whose hand have I accepted a bribe to make me shut my eyes? If I have done any of these things, I will make it right."

"You have not cheated or oppressed us," they replied. "You have not taken anything from anyone's hand."

Samuel said to them, "The LORD is witness against you, and also his anointed is witness this day, that you have not found anything in my hand."

"He is witness," they said.

Then Samuel said to the people, "It is the LORD who appointed Moses and Aaron and brought your ancestors up out of Egypt. Now then, stand here, because I am going to confront you with evidence before the LORD as to all the righteous acts performed by the LORD for you and your ancestors. . . .

"But when you saw that Nahash king of the Ammonites was moving against you, you said to me, 'No, we want a king to rule over us'—even though the LORD your God was your king. Now here is the king you have chosen, the one you asked for; see, the LORD has set a king over you. If you fear the LORD and serve and obey him and do not rebel against his commands, and if both you and the king who reigns over you follow the LORD your God—good! But if you do not obey the LORD, and if you rebel against his commands, his hand will be against you, as it was against your ancestors.

"Now then, stand still and see this great thing the LORD is about to do before your eyes! Is it not wheat harvest now? I will call on the LORD to send thunder and rain. And you will realize what an evil thing you did in the eyes of the LORD when you asked for a king."

Then Samuel called on the LORD, and that same day the LORD sent thunder and rain. So all the people stood in awe of the LORD and of Samuel.

The people all said to Samuel, "Pray to the LORD your God for your servants so that we will not die, for we have added to all our other sins the evil of asking for a king."

"Do not be afraid," Samuel replied. "You have done all this evil; yet do not turn away from the LORD, but serve the LORD with all your heart. Do not turn away after useless idols. They can do you no good, nor can they rescue you, because they are useless. For the sake of his great name the LORD will not reject his people, because the LORD was pleased to make you his own. As for me, far be it from me that I should sin against the LORD by failing to pray for you. And I will teach you the way that is good and right. But be sure to fear the LORD and serve him faithfully with all your heart; consider what great things he has done for you. Yet if you persist in doing evil, both you and your king will perish."

1. *Which is more of a threat to faith in God, good rulers or bad rulers? When our politicians are at their best, are we not more likely to put our confidence in them than in God? What would it mean if America (or any nation) were truly a "Christian nation"? Would that be a good thing or a bad thing?*

2. *Do church leaders today face the temptation to exploit those they lead for power and money? Do national leaders? How rare is it for those in power to be able to say they have cheated no one? What would it mean to have leaders like Samuel?*

3. *The Israelites ask Samuel to intercede with God for them. He says it would be a sin for him not to pray for them (1 Sam. 12:23). How often do we intercede for others, particularly for their forgiveness? Why do we more easily ask for prayer when we are sick than when we have sinned? What is the relationship between honesty, repentance, and intercession?*

Meditation on 1 Samuel 7:3–12; 8:1–9:3; 9:5–6, 15–21; 10:1–11, 17–24; 10:26–12:7; 12:12–12:25

Are we content with God as our leader? Surely our answer would be yes. Israel also would have claimed to be content with God as their ruler; yet to be like the other nations, they requested a king. Even though Samuel warned them of the tyranny a king would bring, they persisted in their request. God gives them a king, Saul, who at first rules wisely, but later proves to be a tyrant.

How foolish of Israel! But are we better? We claim to follow God alone, but we still put our trust in political parties, presidents, and policies. Do we really hear the voice of God who invites us to trust him alone as our ruler? Do we truly know where our citizenship lies? Or, like Israel, do we want God but also want to be like the nations? Do we believe God rules, or do we fear terrorists, criminals, or a failing economy?

The good news in Samuel is that we serve a God who is faithful and loyal to us even when we reject him. He is such a powerful God that he can work his will even through the bad choices of his people. He is a God who always invites us to return to him with our whole heart.

Having seen the Spirit of God at work in Saul, Samuel takes the opportunity at Gilgal to make his farewell address to Israel (although this is not the end of Samuel's work). He begins by defending his actions as leader, calling on Israel to bear witness that he has not enriched himself at their expense. Israel in turn swears before God that Samuel has treated no one unfairly.

Samuel then calls the people to repent. He retells all God had done for them and their ancestors from the time of their deliverance from slavery in Egypt through the years of disobedience and punishment in the wilderness. He reminds them of their unfaithfulness in the time of the judges and recounts God's faithfulness in delivering them when they repented.

He ends with Israel's most recent act of mistrust. They asked for a king instead of trusting in God to deliver. But even now, if Israel and their king will turn to God, he will bless. Samuel ends his warning by calling on the Lord to send thunder and rain to show God's power and his displeasure with Israel. God thunders. In fear, the people confess their sin of asking for a king. They ask Samuel to pray to God for their forgiveness. He agrees to do so, telling them not to fear, for the Lord will not reject his penitent people. God is faithful. He can work his will despite the bad choices his people make.

"God our King, forgive our selfish choices. May we trust in your faithfulness. Your will be done!"

A GOD WHO KNOWS THE HEART

13:5–14; 14:1, 3, 6–30, 36–45;
15:1–3, 7–29, 32–35; 16:1–13 NLT

DAY ONE READING AND QUESTIONS

The Philistines mustered a mighty army of 3,000 chariots, 6,000 charioteers, and as many warriors as the grains of sand on the seashore! They camped at Micmash east of Beth-aven. The men of Israel saw what a tight spot they were in; and because they were hard pressed by the enemy, they tried to hide in caves, thickets, rocks, holes, and cisterns. Some of them crossed the Jordan River and escaped into the land of Gad and Gilead.

Meanwhile, Saul stayed at Gilgal, and his men were trembling with fear. Saul waited there seven days for Samuel, as Samuel had instructed him earlier, but Samuel still didn't come. Saul realized that his troops were rapidly slipping away. So he demanded, "Bring me the burnt offering and the peace offerings!" And Saul sacrificed the burnt offering himself.

Just as Saul was finishing with the burnt offering, Samuel arrived. Saul went out to meet and welcome him, but Samuel said, "What is this you have done?"

Saul replied, "I saw my men scattering from me, and you didn't arrive when you said you would, and the Philistines are at Micmash ready for battle. So I said, 'The Philistines are ready to march against us at Gilgal, and I haven't even asked for the LORD's help!' So I felt compelled to offer the burnt offering myself before you came."

"How foolish!" Samuel exclaimed. "You have not kept the command the LORD your God gave you. Had you kept it, the LORD would have established your kingdom over Israel forever.

But now your kingdom must end, for the LORD has sought out a man after his own heart. The LORD has already appointed him to be the leader of his people, because you have not kept the LORD's command."

1. *What did Saul do to disobey God? Are Samuel and God too harsh on Saul?*

2. *Why didn't Samuel come in the seven days he said he would? Do we (like Saul) have trouble waiting for God?*

3. *Is Saul's fear of the Philistines understandable? After trusting God for victory once, should he not have trusted him here? What is wrong with Saul's heart in this passage? Do we often forget God's deliverance in the past in light of the threats we face today?*

DAY TWO READING AND QUESTIONS

One day Jonathan said to his armor bearer, "Come on, let's go over to where the Philistines have their outpost." But Jonathan did not tell his father what he was doing. . . .

No one realized that Jonathan had left the Israelite camp. . . . "Let's go across to the outpost of those pagans," Jonathan said to his armor bearer. "Perhaps the LORD will help us, for nothing can hinder the LORD. He can win a battle whether he has many warriors or only a few!"

"Do what you think is best," the armor bearer replied. "I'm with you completely, whatever you decide."

"All right, then," Jonathan told him. "We will cross over and let them see us. If they say to us, 'Stay where you are or we'll kill you,' then we will stop and not go up to them. But if they say, 'Come on up and fight,' then we will go up. That will be the LORD's sign that he will help us defeat them."

When the Philistines saw them coming, they shouted, "Look! The Hebrews are crawling out of their holes!" Then the men from the outpost shouted to Jonathan, "Come on up here, and we'll teach you a lesson!"

"Come on, climb right behind me," Jonathan said to his armor bearer, "for the LORD will help us defeat them!"

So they climbed up using both hands and feet, and the Philistines fell before Jonathan, and his armor bearer killed those who came behind them. They killed some twenty men in all, and their bodies were scattered over about half an acre.

Suddenly, panic broke out in the Philistine army, both in the camp and in the field, including even the outposts and raiding parties. And just then an earthquake struck, and everyone was terrified.

Saul's lookouts in Gibeah of Benjamin saw a strange sight—the vast army of Philistines began to melt away in every direction. "Call the roll and find out who's missing," Saul ordered. And when they checked, they found that Jonathan and his armor bearer were gone.

Then Saul shouted to Ahijah, "Bring the ephod here!" For at that time Ahijah was wearing the ephod in front of the Israelites. But while Saul was talking to the priest, the confusion in the Philistine camp grew louder and louder. So Saul said to the priest, "Never mind; let's get going!"

Then Saul and all his men rushed out to the battle and found the Philistines killing each other. There was terrible confusion everywhere. Even the Hebrews who had previously gone over to the Philistine army revolted and joined in with Saul, Jonathan, and the rest of the Israelites. Likewise, the men of Israel who were hiding in the hill country of Ephraim joined the chase when they saw the Philistines running away. So the LORD saved Israel that day, and the battle continued to rage even beyond Beth-aven.

1. *Jonathan believed the Lord could rescue Israel by many or by few. How often do we fail to act against evil because the odds are too overwhelming? Do we rely on our numbers or on God?*

2. *When we win victories over evil, do we give glory to God or to our hard work, strategy, and persistence?*

3. *Who saved Israel, Jonathan or the Lord? How exactly did God work through Jonathan? How does he work through us?*

DAY THREE READING AND QUESTIONS

Now the men of Israel were pressed to exhaustion that day, because Saul had placed them under an oath, saying, "Let a curse fall on anyone who eats before evening—before I have full revenge on my enemies." So no one ate anything all day, even though they had all found honeycomb on the ground in the forest. They didn't dare touch the honey because they all feared the oath they had taken.

But Jonathan had not heard his father's command, and he dipped the end of his stick into a piece of honeycomb and ate the honey. After he had eaten it, he felt refreshed. But one of the men saw him and said, "Your father made the army take a strict oath that anyone who eats food today will be cursed. That is why everyone is weary and faint."

"My father has made trouble for us all!" Jonathan exclaimed. "A command like that only hurts us. See how refreshed I am now that I have eaten this little bit of honey. If the men had been allowed to eat freely from the food they found among our enemies, think how many more Philistines we could have killed!" . . .

Then Saul said, "Let's chase the Philistines all night and plunder them until sunrise. Let's destroy every last one of them."

His men replied, "We'll do whatever you think is best."

But the priest said, "Let's ask God first."

So Saul asked God, "Should we go after the Philistines? Will you help us defeat them?" But God made no reply that day.

Then Saul said to the leaders, "Something's wrong! I want all my army commanders to come here. We must find out what sin was committed today. I vow by the name of the LORD who rescued Israel that the sinner will surely die, even if it is my own son Jonathan!" But no one would tell him what the trouble was.

Then Saul said, "Jonathan and I will stand over here, and all of you stand over there."

And the people responded to Saul, "Whatever you think is best."

Then Saul prayed, "O LORD, God of Israel, please show us who is guilty and who is innocent." Then they cast sacred lots, and Jonathan and Saul were chosen as the guilty ones, and the people were declared innocent.

Then Saul said, "Now cast lots again and choose between me and Jonathan." And Jonathan was shown to be the guilty one.

"Tell me what you have done," Saul demanded of Jonathan.

"I tasted a little honey," Jonathan admitted. "It was only a little bit on the end of my stick. Does that deserve death?"

"Yes, Jonathan," Saul said, "you must die! May God strike me and even kill me if you do not die for this."

> But the people broke in and said to Saul, "Jonathan has won this great victory for Israel. Should he die? Far from it! As surely as the LORD lives, not one hair on his head will be touched, for God helped him do a great deed today." So the people rescued Jonathan, and he was not put to death.

1. *Saul takes an oath to curse anyone who eats before dark. When he proposes to execute Jonathan, isn't he simply trying to keep his oath before God? What's wrong with that?*

2. *Shouldn't we obey God? Can obedience of rules get in the way of having a heart for God?*

3. *What are some ways we make trouble for God's people with our church rules in spite of our good intentions?*

DAY FOUR READING AND QUESTIONS

> One day Samuel said to Saul, "It was the LORD who told me to anoint you as king of his people, Israel. Now listen to this message from the LORD! This is what the LORD of Heaven's Armies has declared: I have decided to settle accounts with the nation of Amalek for opposing Israel when they came from Egypt. Now go and completely destroy the entire Amalekite nation—men, women, children, babies, cattle, sheep, goats, camels, and donkeys." . . .
>
> Then Saul slaughtered the Amalekites from Havilah all the way to Shur, east of Egypt. He captured Agag, the Amalekite king, but completely destroyed everyone else. Saul and his men

spared Agag's life and kept the best of the sheep and goats, the cattle, the fat calves, and the lambs—everything, in fact, that appealed to them. They destroyed only what was worthless or of poor quality.

Then the LORD said to Samuel, "I am sorry that I ever made Saul king, for he has not been loyal to me and has refused to obey my command." Samuel was so deeply moved when he heard this that he cried out to the LORD all night.

Early the next morning Samuel went to find Saul. Someone told him, "Saul went to the town of Carmel to set up a monument to himself; then he went on to Gilgal."

When Samuel finally found him, Saul greeted him cheerfully. "May the LORD bless you," he said. "I have carried out the LORD's command!"

"Then what is all the bleating of sheep and goats and the lowing of cattle I hear?" Samuel demanded.

"It's true that the army spared the best of the sheep, goats, and cattle," Saul admitted. "But they are going to sacrifice them to the LORD your God. We have destroyed everything else."

Then Samuel said to Saul, "Stop! Listen to what the LORD told me last night!"

"What did he tell you?" Saul asked.

And Samuel told him, "Although you may think little of yourself, are you not the leader of the tribes of Israel? The LORD has anointed you king of Israel. And the LORD sent you on a mission and told you, 'Go and completely destroy the sinners, the Amalekites, until they are all dead.' Why haven't you obeyed the LORD? Why did you rush for the plunder and do what was evil in the LORD's sight?"

"But I did obey the LORD," Saul insisted. "I carried out the mission he gave me. I brought back King Agag, but I destroyed everyone else. Then my troops brought in the best of the sheep, goats, cattle, and plunder to sacrifice to the LORD your God in Gilgal."

But Samuel replied,

> "What is more pleasing to the LORD:
> your burnt offerings and sacrifices
> or your obedience to his voice?
> Listen! Obedience is better than sacrifice,
> and submission is better than offering the fat of rams.
> Rebellion is as sinful as witchcraft,
> and stubbornness as bad as worshiping idols.
> So because you have rejected the command of the LORD,
> he has rejected you as king."

Then Saul admitted to Samuel, "Yes, I have sinned. I have disobeyed your instructions and the LORD's command, for I was afraid of the people and did what they demanded. But now, please forgive my sin and come back with me so that I may worship the LORD."

But Samuel replied, "I will not go back with you! Since you have rejected the LORD's command, he has rejected you as king of Israel."

As Samuel turned to go, Saul tried to hold him back and tore the hem of his robe. And Samuel said to him, "The LORD has torn the kingdom of Israel from you today and has given it to someone else—one who is better than you. And he who is the Glory of Israel will not lie, nor will he change his mind, for he is not human that he should change his mind!" . . .

Then Samuel said, "Bring King Agag to me." Agag arrived full of hope, for he thought, "Surely the worst is over, and I have been spared!" But Samuel said, "As your sword has killed the sons of many mothers, now your mother will be childless." And Samuel cut Agag to pieces before the LORD at Gilgal.

Then Samuel went home to Ramah, and Saul returned to his house at Gibeah of Saul. Samuel never went to meet with Saul again, but he mourned constantly for him. And the LORD was sorry he had ever made Saul king of Israel.

1. *Why does Saul disobey? Did he really think he was obeying God? Can we deceive ourselves into thinking we are obeying when we are actually rebelling against God (see Matt. 7:21–23)?*

2. *What is the relationship between listening to God and having a heart like his? What does good-hearted listening look like? Is it related to obedience? Can one obey without a good heart?*

3. *"The LORD was sorry he had ever made Saul king" (1 Sam. 15:35). What does this tell us about God? Does he make mistakes? Can he change his mind? Does his grief have anything to do with human free will? Does it have anything to do with his love for Saul?*

DAY FIVE READING AND QUESTIONS

Now the LORD said to Samuel, "You have mourned long enough for Saul. I have rejected him as king of Israel, so fill your flask with olive oil and go to Bethlehem. Find a man named Jesse who lives there, for I have selected one of his sons to be my king."

But Samuel asked, "How can I do that? If Saul hears about it, he will kill me."

"Take a heifer with you," the LORD replied, "and say that you have come to make a sacrifice to the LORD. Invite Jesse to the sacrifice, and I will show you which of his sons to anoint for me."

So Samuel did as the LORD instructed. When he arrived at Bethlehem, the elders of the town came trembling to meet him. "What's wrong?" they asked. "Do you come in peace?"

"Yes," Samuel replied. "I have come to sacrifice to the LORD. Purify yourselves and come with me to the sacrifice." Then Samuel performed the purification rite for Jesse and his sons and invited them to the sacrifice, too.

When they arrived, Samuel took one look at Eliab and thought, "Surely this is the LORD's anointed!"

But the LORD said to Samuel, "Don't judge by his appearance or height, for I have rejected him. The LORD doesn't see things the way you see them. People judge by outward appearance, but the LORD looks at the heart."

Then Jesse told his son Abinadab to step forward and walk in front of Samuel. But Samuel said, "This is not the one the LORD has chosen." Next Jesse summoned Shimea, but Samuel said, "Neither is this the one the LORD has chosen." In the same way all seven of Jesse's sons were presented to Samuel. But Samuel said to Jesse, "The LORD has not chosen any of these." Then Samuel asked, "Are these all the sons you have?"

"There is still the youngest," Jesse replied. "But he's out in the fields watching the sheep and goats."

"Send for him at once," Samuel said. "We will not sit down to eat until he arrives."

So Jesse sent for him. He was dark and handsome, with beautiful eyes.

And the LORD said, "This is the one; anoint him."

So as David stood there among his brothers, Samuel took the flask of olive oil he had brought and anointed David with the oil. And the Spirit of the LORD came powerfully upon David from that day on. Then Samuel returned to Ramah.

1. *What are some ways we judge others by appearance? Do we pick our political leaders this way? Our church leaders? God judges the heart. Can we? What are some ways we can know what is in someone's heart?*

2. *What does it mean to be a person after God's own heart? What is the heart of God? What attitudes and actions come from that heart? How can we have the heart of God?*

3. *What is the relation between having the heart of God and the Holy Spirit? Did Saul have the Spirit? Does he possess the Spirit in these chapters (1 Sam. 13–15)?*

Meditation on 1 Samuel 13:5–14; 14:1, 3, 6–30, 36–45; 15:1–3, 7–29, 32–35; 16:1–13

Earlier Saul had heard the voice of God. He was filled with the Spirit and numbered among the prophets (1 Sam. 10:9–11). He wins his great victory over the Ammonites at Jabesh Gilead by trusting in the power of the Lord, refusing to take the credit for himself (1 Sam. 11:13).

But he will not continue to listen for God's voice. In this section, he will not wait on the prophet of the Lord but instead offers the sacrifice on his own. He makes foolish rules for his army, causing the Lord to refuse to answer him. Believing he has a better plan, Saul even directly disobeys God's instructions regarding the Amalekites. Since Saul stops listening to God, the Lord rejects him as king and turns to another who will welcome the Spirit of the Lord.

God sends Samuel to anoint a new king, a son of Jesse. Samuel does not announce his intention, out of fear of Saul, but tells the elders of

Bethlehem he has come to sacrifice. Inviting Jesse and his family to the sacrifice, Samuel is impressed with Eliab, Jesse's oldest son, and is sure this is the one God has chosen as king.

The Lord replies, "The LORD does not look at the things people look at. People look at the outward appearance, but the LORD looks at the heart" (1 Sam. 16:7 NIV). Jesse parades all his sons before Samuel, but the Lord chooses none of them. Finally, the youngest son, David, arrives from the field. The Lord says, "He is the one," so Samuel anoints him. The Spirit of the Lord then comes upon David with power. God has found "a man after his own heart" (1 Sam. 13:14).

Still today, the Lord looks not at outward appearance but at hearts that are willing to turn to him.

"God of love, send your Spirit to us today so we may have hearts like yours."

A GOD WHO DELIVERS

16:14–23; 17:4–11, 17–29, 32–51; 18:1–19:7; 19:9–24 NIV

DAY ONE READING AND QUESTIONS

Now the Spirit of the LORD had departed from Saul, and an evil spirit from the LORD tormented him.

Saul's attendants said to him, "See, an evil spirit from God is tormenting you. Let our lord command his servants here to search for someone who can play the lyre. He will play when the evil spirit from God comes on you, and you will feel better."

So Saul said to his attendants, "Find someone who plays well and bring him to me."

One of the servants answered, "I have seen a son of Jesse of Bethlehem who knows how to play the lyre. He is a brave man and a warrior. He speaks well and is a fine-looking man. And the LORD is with him."

Then Saul sent messengers to Jesse and said, "Send me your son David, who is with the sheep." So Jesse took a donkey loaded with bread, a skin of wine and a young goat and sent them with his son David to Saul.

David came to Saul and entered his service. Saul liked him very much, and David became one of his armor-bearers. Then Saul sent word to Jesse, saying, "Allow David to remain in my service, for I am pleased with him."

Whenever the spirit from God came on Saul, David would take up his lyre and play. Then relief would come to Saul; he would feel better, and the evil spirit would leave him.

1. *Can one truly be neutral when it comes to God? If one does not have God's Spirit, what kind of spirit takes over?*

2. *How does one hold on to the presence of the Spirit?*

3. *When has God worked his will in your life through what seemed at the time like insignificant choices?*

DAY TWO READING AND QUESTIONS

A champion named Goliath, who was from Gath, came out of the Philistine camp. His height was six cubits and a span. He had a bronze helmet on his head and wore a coat of scale armor of bronze weighing five thousand shekels; on his legs he wore bronze greaves, and a bronze javelin was slung on his back. His spear shaft was like a weaver's rod, and its iron point weighed six hundred shekels. His shield bearer went ahead of him.

Goliath stood and shouted to the ranks of Israel, "Why do you come out and line up for battle? Am I not a Philistine, and are you not the servants of Saul? Choose a man and have him come down to me. If he is able to fight and kill me, we will become your subjects; but if I overcome him and kill him, you will become our subjects and serve us." Then the Philistine said, "This day I defy the armies of Israel! Give me a man and let us fight each other." On hearing the Philistine's words, Saul and all the Israelites were dismayed and terrified. . . .

Now Jesse said to his son David, "Take this ephah of roasted grain and these ten loaves of bread for your brothers and hurry to their camp. Take along these ten cheeses to the commander of their unit. See how your brothers are and bring back some assurance from them. They are with Saul and all the men of Israel in the Valley of Elah, fighting against the Philistines."

Early in the morning David left the flock in the care of a shepherd, loaded up and set out, as Jesse had directed. He reached the camp as the army was going out to its battle positions, shouting the war cry. Israel and the Philistines were drawing up their lines facing each other. David left his things with the keeper of supplies, ran to the battle lines and asked his brothers how they were. As he was talking with them, Goliath, the Philistine champion from Gath, stepped out from his lines and shouted his usual defiance, and David heard it. Whenever the Israelites saw the man, they all fled from him in great fear.

Now the Israelites had been saying, "Do you see how this man keeps coming out? He comes out to defy Israel. The king will give great wealth to the man who kills him. He will also give him his daughter in marriage and will exempt his family from taxes in Israel."

David asked the men standing near him, "What will be done for the man who kills this Philistine and removes this disgrace from Israel? Who is this uncircumcised Philistine that he should defy the armies of the living God?"

They repeated to him what they had been saying and told him, "This is what will be done for the man who kills him."

When Eliab, David's oldest brother, heard him speaking with the men, he burned with anger at him and asked, "Why have you come down here? And with whom did you leave those few sheep in the wilderness? I know how conceited you are and how wicked your heart is; you came down only to watch the battle."

"Now what have I done?" said David. "Can't I even speak?" . . .

David said to Saul, "Let no one lose heart on account of this Philistine; your servant will go and fight him."

Saul replied, "You are not able to go out against this Philistine and fight him; you are only a young man, and he has been a warrior from his youth."

But David said to Saul, "Your servant has been keeping his father's sheep. When a lion or a bear came and carried off a sheep from the flock, I went after it, struck it and rescued the sheep from its mouth. When it turned on me, I seized it by its hair, struck it and killed it. Your servant has killed both the lion and the bear; this uncircumcised Philistine will be like one of them, because he has defied the armies of the living God. The LORD who rescued me from the paw of the lion and the paw of the bear will rescue me from the hand of this Philistine."

Saul said to David, "Go, and the LORD be with you."

Then Saul dressed David in his own tunic. He put a coat of armor on him and a bronze helmet on his head. David fastened on his sword over the tunic and tried walking around, because he was not used to them.

"I cannot go in these," he said to Saul, "because I am not used to them." So he took them off. Then he took his staff in his hand, chose five smooth stones from the stream, put them in the pouch of his shepherd's bag and, with his sling in his hand, approached the Philistine.

Meanwhile, the Philistine, with his shield bearer in front of him, kept coming closer to David. He looked David over and saw that he was little more than a boy, glowing with health and handsome, and he despised him. He said to David, "Am I a dog, that you come at me with sticks?" And the Philistine cursed David by his gods. "Come here," he said, "and I'll give your flesh to the birds and the wild animals!"

David said to the Philistine, "You come against me with sword and spear and javelin, but I come against you in the name of the LORD Almighty, the God of the armies of Israel, whom you have defied. This day the LORD will deliver you into my hands, and I'll strike you down and cut off your head. This very day I will give the carcasses of the Philistine army to the birds and the wild animals, and the whole world will know that there is a God in Israel. All those gathered here will know that it is not by sword or spear that the LORD saves; for the battle is the LORD's, and he will give all of you into our hands."

As the Philistine moved closer to attack him, David ran quickly toward the battle line to meet him. Reaching into his bag and taking out a stone, he slung it and struck the Philistine on the forehead. The stone sank into his forehead, and he fell facedown on the ground.

So David triumphed over the Philistine with a sling and a stone; without a sword in his hand he struck down the Philistine and killed him.

David ran and stood over him. He took hold of the Philistine's sword and drew it from the sheath. After he killed him, he cut off his head with the sword.

When the Philistines saw that their hero was dead, they turned and ran.

1. *David not only has to fight Goliath but also the ridicule and skepticism of his own family and nation. Which is harder to fight? Do those closest to us sometimes get in the way when we try to hear God? How?*

2. *Like Saul, do we sometimes send others to fight our battles for us?*

3. *Is our reliance on preachers, elders, and other church leaders an example of faith or distrust in God? Are we willing to trust God alone in our battles, or do we trust in our abilities or others' leadership?*

DAY THREE READING AND QUESTIONS

After David had finished talking with Saul, Jonathan became one in spirit with David, and he loved him as himself. From that day Saul kept David with him and did not let him return home to his family. And Jonathan made a covenant with David because he loved him as himself. Jonathan took off the robe he was wearing and gave it to David, along with his tunic, and even his sword, his bow and his belt.

Whatever mission Saul sent him on, David was so successful that Saul gave him a high rank in the army. This pleased all the troops, and Saul's officers as well.

When the men were returning home after David had killed the Philistine, the women came out from all the towns of Israel to meet King Saul with singing and dancing, with joyful songs and with timbrels and lyres. As they danced, they sang:

> "Saul has slain his thousands,
> and David his tens of thousands."

Saul was very angry; this refrain displeased him greatly. "They have credited David with tens of thousands," he thought, "but me with only thousands. What more can he get but the kingdom?" And from that time on Saul kept a close eye on David.

The next day an evil spirit from God came forcefully on Saul. He was prophesying in his house, while David was playing the lyre, as he usually did. Saul had a spear in his hand and he hurled it, saying to himself, "I'll pin David to the wall." But David eluded him twice.

Saul was afraid of David, because the LORD was with David but had departed from Saul. So he sent David away from him and gave him command over a thousand men, and David led the troops in their campaigns. In everything he did he had great success, because the LORD was with him. When Saul saw how successful he was, he was afraid of him. But all Israel and Judah loved David, because he led them in their campaigns.

Saul said to David, "Here is my older daughter Merab. I will give her to you in marriage; only serve me bravely and fight the battles of the LORD." For Saul said to himself, "I will not raise a hand against him. Let the Philistines do that!"

But David said to Saul, "Who am I, and what is my family or my clan in Israel, that I should become the king's son-in-law?" So when the time came for Merab, Saul's daughter, to be given to David, she was given in marriage to Adriel of Meholah.

Now Saul's daughter Michal was in love with David, and when they told Saul about it, he was pleased. "I will give her to him," he thought, "so that she may be a snare to him and so that the hand of the Philistines may be against him." So Saul said to David, "Now you have a second opportunity to become my son-in-law."

Then Saul ordered his attendants: "Speak to David privately and say, 'Look, the king likes you, and his attendants all love you; now become his son-in-law.'"

They repeated these words to David. But David said, "Do you think it is a small matter to become the king's son-in-law? I'm only a poor man and little known."

When Saul's servants told him what David had said, Saul replied, "Say to David, 'The king wants no other price for the bride than a hundred Philistine foreskins, to take revenge on his enemies.'" Saul's plan was to have David fall by the hands of the Philistines.

When the attendants told David these things, he was pleased to become the king's son-in-law. So before the allotted time elapsed, David took his men with him and went out and killed two hundred Philistines and brought back their foreskins. They counted out the full number to the king so that David might become the king's son-in-law. Then Saul gave him his daughter Michal in marriage.

When Saul realized that the Lord was with David and that his daughter Michal loved David, Saul became still more afraid of him, and he remained his enemy the rest of his days.

The Philistine commanders continued to go out to battle, and as often as they did, David met with more success than the rest of Saul's officers, and his name became well known.

1. *Have you ever been jealous of someone because they were better than you? Does that jealousy usually spring from fear? How?*

2. *Do others sometimes hate us because of our relationship with God? Did this happen to Jesus? Is this what Jesus meant when he warned his followers they would be persecuted?*

3. *How should we treat those who are jealous of us? How did David? How did Jesus?*

DAY FOUR READING AND QUESTIONS

Saul told his son Jonathan and all the attendants to kill David. But Jonathan had taken a great liking to David and warned him,

"My father Saul is looking for a chance to kill you. Be on your guard tomorrow morning; go into hiding and stay there. I will go out and stand with my father in the field where you are. I'll speak to him about you and will tell you what I find out."

Jonathan spoke well of David to Saul his father and said to him, "Let not the king do wrong to his servant David; he has not wronged you, and what he has done has benefited you greatly. He took his life in his hands when he killed the Philistine. The LORD won a great victory for all Israel, and you saw it and were glad. Why then would you do wrong to an innocent man like David by killing him for no reason?"

Saul listened to Jonathan and took this oath: "As surely as the LORD lives, David will not be put to death."

So Jonathan called David and told him the whole conversation. He brought him to Saul, and David was with Saul as before. . . .

But an evil spirit from the LORD came on Saul as he was sitting in his house with his spear in his hand. While David was playing the lyre, Saul tried to pin him to the wall with his spear, but David eluded him as Saul drove the spear into the wall. That night David made good his escape.

Saul sent men to David's house to watch it and to kill him in the morning. But Michal, David's wife, warned him, "If you don't run for your life tonight, tomorrow you'll be killed." So Michal let David down through a window, and he fled and escaped. Then Michal took an idol and laid it on the bed, covering it with a garment and putting some goats' hair at the head.

When Saul sent the men to capture David, Michal said, "He is ill."

Then Saul sent the men back to see David and told them, "Bring him up to me in his bed so that I may kill him." But when the men entered, there was the idol in the bed, and at the head was some goats' hair.

Saul said to Michal, "Why did you deceive me like this and send my enemy away so that he escaped?"

Michal told him, "He said to me, 'Let me get away. Why should I kill you?'"

When David had fled and made his escape, he went to Samuel at Ramah and told him all that Saul had done to him. Then he and Samuel went to Naioth and stayed there. Word came to Saul: "David is in Naioth at Ramah"; so he sent men to capture him. But when they saw a group of prophets prophesying, with Samuel standing there as their leader, the Spirit of God came on Saul's men, and they also prophesied. Saul was told about it, and he sent more men, and they prophesied too. Saul sent men a third time, and they also prophesied. Finally, he himself left for Ramah and went to the great cistern at Seku. And he asked, "Where are Samuel and David?"

"Over in Naioth at Ramah," they said.

So Saul went to Naioth at Ramah. But the Spirit of God came even on him, and he walked along prophesying until he came to Naioth. He stripped off his garments, and he too prophesied in Samuel's presence. He lay naked all that day and all that night. This is why people say, "Is Saul also among the prophets?"

1. *Why do Jonathan and Michal go against their father's wishes and rescue David? What does this say about them? About Saul? About David? About God?*

2. *God rescues David by temporarily making Saul a prophet. What does "prophesying" mean in this passage?*

3. *Can one be a prophet and still not be right with God? Do gifts from God and his Spirit guarantee that those who receive the gifts are right with God?*

DAY FIVE READING AND QUESTIONS

Go back and read 1 Samuel 16:14–23; 17:4–11, 17–29, 32–51; 18:1–19:7; 19:9–24.

1. *In this section, Saul is constantly afraid while David and Jonathan are bold and fearless. Is fear the greatest threat to Christians today? What are we afraid of? Why are we afraid?*

2. *If we truly trusted God, would our fears disappear?*

3. *Think of all the ways God delivers David in this section. How has he delivered you in the past? Through friends? Family? Church? Circumstances? Share those deliverances with others.*

Meditation on 1 Samuel 16:14–23; 17:4–11, 17–29, 32–51; 18:1–19:7; 19:9–24

It's one of the most famous stories in the Bible, a story most of us heard as children. We could relate to those who feared a giant, because everyone seemed nine-foot tall to us. Even now as adults, we might feel small in the face of our challengers. Most today use the story of David and Goliath as a proverbial lesson on the triumph of the underdog.

But the story is much more than that. Like the rest of Samuel, it is a story of listening to God or rejecting him, of faith versus fear. Goliath defies the God of Israel, but the army of Israel along with King Saul are "dismayed and terrified" by his defiant words (1 Sam. 17:11). David comes on the scene, too young to join the army and unskilled in battle. All David has is faith in the God who has been his deliverer. "The LORD who rescued me from the paw of the lion and the paw of the bear will rescue me from the hand of this Philistine" (1 Sam. 17:37). Saul, who does not trust God enough to fight Goliath himself, is willing for David to fight, saying, "Go, and the LORD be with you."

Goliath sees David coming and despises him, thinking him an unworthy opponent—a young, unproven warrior with no weapon but a sling. But David brings out the big weapon: the name of the Lord.

And the Lord delivers David.

To whom are we listening? To the Goliaths inside and outside of us? To those loud voices of temptation, selfishness, greed, and hatred? Or, like David, are our hearts and ears tuned to the voice of the One who promises us victory in battle?

It's very hard to hear the voice of God in the face of giants who oppose us. Our fears drown out God's voice. David can hear the promises of God in the face of overwhelming odds. Saul cannot hear, for the Lord has left him. David's faith leads to victory. Saul's fear leads to cowardly defeat. Are we willing to listen to the voice of God above the din of our fears?

"God of power, give us courage when we are afraid. May we always rely on your strength, not our own."

A GOD OF FRIENDSHIP

20:3–23; 20:35–21:9; 22:9–19; 23:1–14; 24:1–22 NLT

DAY ONE READING AND QUESTIONS

Then David took an oath before Jonathan and said, "Your father knows perfectly well about our friendship, so he has said to himself, 'I won't tell Jonathan—why should I hurt him?' But I swear to you that I am only a step away from death! I swear it by the LORD and by your own soul!"

"Tell me what I can do to help you," Jonathan exclaimed.

David replied, "Tomorrow we celebrate the new moon festival. I've always eaten with the king on this occasion, but tomorrow I'll hide in the field and stay there until the evening of the third day. If your father asks where I am, tell him I asked permission to go home to Bethlehem for an annual family sacrifice. If he says, 'Fine!' you will know all is well. But if he is angry and loses his temper, you will know he is determined to kill me. Show me this loyalty as my sworn friend—for we made a solemn pact before the LORD—or kill me yourself if I have sinned against your father. But please don't betray me to him!"

"Never!" Jonathan exclaimed. "You know that if I had the slightest notion my father was planning to kill you, I would tell you at once."

Then David asked, "How will I know whether or not your father is angry?"

"Come out to the field with me," Jonathan replied. And they went out there together. Then Jonathan told David, "I promise by the LORD, the God of Israel, that by this time tomorrow, or the next day at the latest, I will talk to my father and let you know at once how he feels about you. If he speaks favorably about you, I will let you know. But if he is angry and wants you killed, may the Lord strike me and even kill me if I don't warn you so you can escape and live. May the Lord be with you as he used to be with my father. And may you treat me with the faithful love of the Lord as long as I live. But if I die, treat my family with this faithful love, even when the Lord destroys all your enemies from the face of the earth."

So Jonathan made a solemn pact with David, saying, "May the Lord destroy all your enemies!" And Jonathan made David reaffirm his vow of friendship again, for Jonathan loved David as he loved himself.

Then Jonathan said, "Tomorrow we celebrate the new moon festival. You will be missed when your place at the table is empty. The day after tomorrow, toward evening, go to the place where you hid before, and wait there by the stone pile. I will come out and shoot three arrows to the side of the stone pile as though I were shooting at a target. Then I will send a boy to bring the arrows back. If you hear me tell him, 'They're on this side,' then you will know, as surely as the Lord lives, that all is well, and there is no trouble. But if I tell him, 'Go farther—the arrows are still ahead of you,' then it will mean that you must leave immediately, for the Lord is sending you away. And may the Lord make us keep our promises to each other, for he has witnessed them." . . .

The next morning, as agreed, Jonathan went out into the field and took a young boy with him to gather his arrows. "Start running," he told the boy, "so you can find the arrows as I shoot them." So the boy ran, and Jonathan shot an arrow beyond him. When the boy had almost reached the arrow, Jonathan shouted, "The arrow is still ahead of you. Hurry, hurry, don't wait." So the boy quickly gathered up the arrows and ran back to his master. He, of course, suspected nothing; only Jonathan and David understood the signal. Then Jonathan gave his bow and arrows to the boy and told him to take them back to town.

As soon as the boy was gone, David came out from where he had been hiding near the stone pile. Then David bowed three times to Jonathan with his face to the ground. Both of them were in tears as they embraced each other and said good-bye, especially David.

At last Jonathan said to David, "Go in peace, for we have sworn loyalty to each other in the LORD's name. The LORD is the witness of a bond between us and our children forever." Then David left, and Jonathan returned to the town.

1. *What are some of the costly friendships you have had? What are we tempted to do when friendship becomes costly and inconvenient?*

2. *What is more important, friendship or family? What happens when we have to choose between them?*

3. *What are the differences between ordinary human friendship and spiritual friendship in terms of the basis of friendship, the goals of friendship, and the lasting nature of friendship?*

DAY TWO READING AND QUESTIONS

David went to the town of Nob to see Ahimelech the priest. Ahimelech trembled when he saw him. "Why are you alone?" he asked. "Why is no one with you?"

"The king has sent me on a private matter," David said. "He told me not to tell anyone why I am here. I have told my men where to meet me later. Now, what is there to eat? Give me five loaves of bread or anything else you have."

"We don't have any regular bread," the priest replied. "But there is the holy bread, which you can have if your young men have not slept with any women recently."

"Don't worry," David replied. "I never allow my men to be with women when we are on a campaign. And since they stay clean even on ordinary trips, how much more on this one!"

Since there was no other food available, the priest gave him the holy bread—the Bread of the Presence that was placed before the LORD in the Tabernacle. It had just been replaced that day with fresh bread.

Now Doeg the Edomite, Saul's chief herdsman, was there that day, having been detained before the LORD.

David asked Ahimelech, "Do you have a spear or sword? The king's business was so urgent that I didn't even have time to grab a weapon!"

"I only have the sword of Goliath the Philistine, whom you killed in the valley of Elah," the priest replied. "It is wrapped in a cloth behind the ephod. Take that if you want it, for there is nothing else here."

"There is nothing like it!" David replied. "Give it to me!"

1. *Is it right to lie to preserve one's life? Does David lie to Ahimelech?*

2. *Is it right to lie to preserve another's life?*

3. *David breaks God's law that said only the priests should eat the consecrated bread. Why does God allow this? Does this say something about the purpose of God's laws (see Matt. 12:1–8)?*

DAY THREE READING AND QUESTIONS

Then Doeg the Edomite, who was standing there with Saul's men, spoke up. "When I was at Nob," he said, "I saw the son of Jesse talking to the priest, Ahimelech son of Ahitub. Ahimelech consulted the LORD for him. Then he gave him food and the sword of Goliath the Philistine."

King Saul immediately sent for Ahimelech and all his family, who served as priests at Nob. When they arrived, Saul shouted at him, "Listen to me, you son of Ahitub!"

"What is it, my king?" Ahimelech asked.

"Why have you and the son of Jesse conspired against me?" Saul demanded. "Why did you give him food and a sword? Why have you consulted God for him? Why have you encouraged him to kill me, as he is trying to do this very day?"

"But sir," Ahimelech replied, "is anyone among all your servants as faithful as David, your son-in-law? Why, he is the captain of your bodyguard and a highly honored member of your household! This was certainly not the first time I had consulted God for him! May the king not accuse me and my family in this matter, for I knew nothing at all of any plot against you."

"You will surely die, Ahimelech, along with your entire family!" the king shouted. And he ordered his bodyguards, "Kill these priests of the LORD, for they are allies and conspirators with David! They knew he was running away from me, but they didn't tell me!" But Saul's men refused to kill the LORD's priests.

Then the king said to Doeg, "You do it." So Doeg the Edomite turned on them and killed them that day, eighty-five priests in all, still wearing their priestly garments. Then he went to Nob, the town of the priests, and killed the priests' families—men and women, children and babies—and all the cattle, donkeys, sheep, and goats.

1. *How much loyalty should we give a king (or a president) even in time of war? What if the ruler is unjust? Can one be loyal to a country and still oppose its policies when they oppress the innocent?*

2. *Saul seems most angry that Ahimelech consulted God for David. He reacts with anger because God had left him but was still with David. Do we sometimes get angry at others because they are more spiritual than we are? How do we show that anger?*

3. *What is the relationship between Saul's fear and his anger? Between our anger and our fear?*

DAY FOUR READING AND QUESTIONS

One day news came to David that the Philistines were at Keilah stealing grain from the threshing floors. David asked the LORD, "Should I go and attack them?"

"Yes, go and save Keilah," the LORD told him.

But David's men said, "We're afraid even here in Judah. We certainly don't want to go to Keilah to fight the whole Philistine army!"

So David asked the LORD again, and again the LORD replied, "Go down to Keilah, for I will help you conquer the Philistines."

So David and his men went to Keilah. They slaughtered the Philistines and took all their livestock and rescued the people of Keilah. Now when Abiathar son of Ahimelech fled to David at Keilah, he brought the ephod with him.

Saul soon learned that David was at Keilah. "Good!" he exclaimed. "We've got him now! God has handed him over to me, for he has trapped himself in a walled town!" So Saul mobilized his entire army to march to Keilah and besiege David and his men.

But David learned of Saul's plan and told Abiathar the priest to bring the ephod and ask the LORD what he should do. Then David prayed, "O LORD, God of Israel, I have heard that Saul is planning to come and destroy Keilah because I am here. Will the leaders of Keilah betray me to him? And will Saul actually come as I have heard? O LORD, God of Israel, please tell me."

And the LORD said, "He will come."

Again David asked, "Will the leaders of Keilah betray me and my men to Saul?"

And the LORD replied, "Yes, they will betray you."

So David and his men—about 600 of them now—left Keilah and began roaming the countryside. Word soon reached Saul that David had escaped, so he didn't go to Keilah after all. David now stayed in the strongholds of the wilderness and in the hill country of Ziph. Saul hunted him day after day, but God didn't let Saul find him.

1. *Do we take the time to inquire of the Lord before we go out to do great things for him? Should Christians and churches spend more time in prayer than they do in planning?*

2. *How has the Lord answered your inquiries in the past? Does he always answer when we expect him to?*

3. *What are ways we can make it easier to hear God's answers?*

DAY FIVE READING AND QUESTIONS

After Saul returned from fighting the Philistines, he was told that David had gone into the wilderness of En-gedi. So Saul chose 3,000 elite troops from all Israel and went to search for David and his men near the rocks of the wild goats.

At the place where the road passes some sheepfolds, Saul went into a cave to relieve himself. But as it happened, David and his men were hiding farther back in that very cave!

"Now's your opportunity!" David's men whispered to him. "Today the LORD is telling you, 'I will certainly put your enemy into your power, to do with as you wish.'" So David crept forward and cut off a piece of the hem of Saul's robe.

But then David's conscience began bothering him because he had cut Saul's robe. He said to his men, "The LORD forbid that I should do this to my lord the king. I shouldn't attack the LORD's anointed one, for the LORD himself has chosen him." So David restrained his men and did not let them kill Saul.

After Saul had left the cave and gone on his way, David came out and shouted after him, "My lord the king!" And when Saul looked around, David bowed low before him.

Then he shouted to Saul, "Why do you listen to the people who say I am trying to harm you? This very day you can see with your own eyes it isn't true. For the LORD placed you at my mercy back there in the cave. Some of my men told me to kill you, but I spared you. For I said, 'I will never harm the king—he is the LORD's anointed one.' Look, my father, at what I have in my hand. It is a piece of the hem of your robe! I cut it off, but I didn't kill you. This proves that I am not trying to harm you and that I have not sinned against you, even though you have been hunting for me to kill me.

"May the LORD judge between us. Perhaps the LORD will punish you for what you are trying to do to me, but I will never harm you. As that old proverb says, 'From evil people come evil deeds.' So you can be sure I will never harm you. Who is the king of Israel trying to catch anyway? Should he spend his time chasing one who is as worthless as a dead dog or a single flea? May the LORD therefore judge which of us is right and punish the guilty one. He is my advocate, and he will rescue me from your power!"

When David had finished speaking, Saul called back, "Is that really you, my son David?" Then he began to cry. And he said to David, "You are a better man than I am, for you have repaid me good for evil. Yes, you have been amazingly kind to me today, for when the LORD put me in a place where you could have killed me, you didn't do it. Who else would let his enemy get away when he had him in his power? May the LORD reward you well for the kindness you have shown me today. And now I realize that you are surely going to be king, and that the kingdom of Israel will flourish under your rule. Now swear to me by the LORD that when that happens you will not kill my family and destroy my line of descendants!"

So David promised this to Saul with an oath. Then Saul went home, but David and his men went back to their stronghold.

1. *Like David, should we have compassion on our enemies? Does that mean we excuse their actions? What about self-defense? Didn't David need to kill Saul to protect himself?*

2. *Should we want God to take vengeance on our enemies? Should we want God to forgive those who persist in ignoring him and in harming others?*

3. *Who is stronger, Saul or David? Does David's compassion toward Saul put him in a weaker position? A more dangerous position? Why are we reluctant to make ourselves vulnerable to others?*

Meditation on 1 Samuel 20:3–23; 20:35–21:9; 22:9–19; 23:1–14; 24:1–22

Once there were two young men. One was the crown prince of the land; the other a humble shepherd. Despite the differences in their upbringing, they got along famously. Day after day, they played and hunted and talked together. They were closer to each other than to their own brothers.

But politics got in their way. The shepherd boy was anointed to be the next king. The prince was not jealous—he was happy for his friend to be king; but the prince's father determined to kill the shepherd boy. The prince heard of the plot and went to warn his friend.

The king's spies made that difficult. The prince didn't know whom he could trust, so he planned a secret code with the shepherd boy. "Tomorrow, I'll go target practicing with my bow and arrow," said the prince. "You hide near the target. If my father has cooled down and things are safe for you, I'll tell my servant, 'The arrows are on this side of you.' If my father is still angry, I'll say, 'The arrows are beyond you,' and you'll know to get out of town."

The code worked. The king was still angry, but the shepherd boy was warned. He had to flee for his life, perhaps never to see the young prince again. But he couldn't leave without saying good-bye.

The two friends—Jonathan and David—embraced and wept, "but David wept the most." No wonder, in light of all Jonathan gave up to be his friend.

But this is more than a story of human friendship. It is the story of the faithfulness of God. He protected his anointed one, David, through the noble friendship of Jonathan.

What is more, David even showed friendship to Saul, the one trying to kill him, by sparing his life.

God sometimes speaks to our hearts most clearly through the words and actions of our friends. The Lord showed his protective care to David through the unselfish life of Jonathan. Think of what it cost for Jonathan to be a friend to David. With David out of the way (as Saul wants), Jonathan would be king of Israel. But Jonathan generously gives up wealth, power, and privilege to be David's friend. Surely God speaks to us today through those godly friends who put our welfare above their own.

"God of friendship, thank you for the friends who lead us to you. May we be that kind of friend to them."

WHEN GOD WILL NOT SPEAK

25:1–26:25; 28:4–20; 29:11–30:25; 31:1–13 NIV

DAY ONE READING AND QUESTIONS

Now Samuel died, and all Israel assembled and mourned for him; and they buried him at his home in Ramah. Then David moved down into the Desert of Paran.

A certain man in Maon, who had property there at Carmel, was very wealthy. He had a thousand goats and three thousand sheep, which he was shearing in Carmel. His name was Nabal and his wife's name was Abigail. She was an intelligent and beautiful woman, but her husband was surly and mean in his dealings—he was a Calebite.

While David was in the wilderness, he heard that Nabal was shearing sheep. So he sent ten young men and said to them, "Go up to Nabal at Carmel and greet him in my name. Say to him: 'Long life to you! Good health to you and your household! And good health to all that is yours!

"'Now I hear that it is sheep-shearing time. When your shepherds were with us, we did not mistreat them, and the whole time they were at Carmel nothing of theirs was missing. Ask your own servants and they will tell you. Therefore be favorable toward my men, since we come at a festive time. Please give your servants and your son David whatever you can find for them.'"

When David's men arrived, they gave Nabal this message in David's name. Then they waited.

Nabal answered David's servants, "Who is this David? Who is this son of Jesse? Many servants are breaking away from their masters these days. Why should I take my bread and water, and the meat I have slaughtered for my shearers, and give it to men coming from who knows where?"

David's men turned around and went back. When they arrived, they reported every word. David said to his men, "Each of you strap on your sword!" So they did, and David strapped his on as well. About four hundred men went up with David, while two hundred stayed with the supplies.

One of the servants told Abigail, Nabal's wife, "David sent messengers from the wilderness to give our master his greetings, but he hurled insults at them. Yet these men were very good to us. They did not mistreat us, and the whole time we were out in the fields near them nothing was missing. Night and day they were a wall around us the whole time we were herding our sheep near them. Now think it over and see what you can do, because disaster is hanging over our master and his whole household. He is such a wicked man that no one can talk to him."

Abigail acted quickly. She took two hundred loaves of bread, two skins of wine, five dressed sheep, five seahs of roasted grain, a hundred cakes of raisins and two hundred cakes of pressed figs, and loaded them on donkeys. Then she told her servants, "Go on ahead; I'll follow you." But she did not tell her husband Nabal.

As she came riding her donkey into a mountain ravine, there were David and his men descending toward her, and she met them. David had just said, "It's been useless—all my watching over this fellow's property in the wilderness so that nothing of his was missing. He has paid me back evil for good. May God deal with David, be it ever so severely, if by morning I leave alive one male of all who belong to him!"

When Abigail saw David, she quickly got off her donkey and bowed down before David with her face to the ground. She fell at his feet and said: "Pardon your servant, my lord, and let me speak to you; hear what your servant has to say. Please pay no attention, my lord, to that wicked man Nabal. He is just like his name—his name means Fool, and folly goes with him. And as for me, your servant, I did not see the men my lord sent. And now, my lord, as surely as the LORD your God lives and as you live, since the LORD has kept you from bloodshed and from avenging yourself with your own hands, may your enemies and all who are intent on harming my lord be like Nabal. And let this gift, which your servant has brought to my lord, be given to the men who follow you.

"Please forgive your servant's presumption. The LORD your God will certainly make a lasting dynasty for my lord, because you fight the LORD's battles, and no wrongdoing will be found in you as long as you live. Even though someone is pursuing you to take your life, the life of my lord will be bound securely in the bundle of the living by the LORD your God, but the lives of your enemies he will hurl away as from the pocket of a sling. When the LORD has fulfilled for my lord every good thing he promised concerning him and has appointed him ruler over Israel, my lord will not have on his conscience the staggering burden of needless bloodshed or of having avenged himself. And when the LORD your God has brought my lord success, remember your servant."

David said to Abigail, "Praise be to the LORD, the God of Israel, who has sent you today to meet me. May you be blessed for your good judgment and for keeping me from bloodshed this day and from avenging myself with my own hands. Otherwise, as surely as the LORD, the God of Israel, lives, who has kept me from harming you, if you had not come quickly to meet me, not one male belonging to Nabal would have been left alive by daybreak."

Then David accepted from her hand what she had brought him and said, "Go home in peace. I have heard your words and granted your request."

When Abigail went to Nabal, he was in the house holding a banquet like that of a king. He was in high spirits and very drunk. So she told him nothing at all until daybreak. Then in the morning, when Nabal was sober, his wife told him all these things, and his heart failed him and he became like a stone. About ten days later, the LORD struck Nabal and he died.

When David heard that Nabal was dead, he said, "Praise be to the LORD, who has upheld my cause against Nabal for treating me with contempt. He has kept his servant from doing wrong and has brought Nabal's wrongdoing down on his own head."

Then David sent word to Abigail, asking her to become his wife. His servants went to Carmel and said to Abigail, "David has sent us to you to take you to become his wife."

She bowed down with her face to the ground and said, "I am your servant and am ready to serve you and wash the feet of my lord's servants." Abigail quickly got on a donkey and, attended by her five female servants, went with David's messengers and became his wife. David had also married Ahinoam of Jezreel, and they both were his wives. But Saul had given his daughter Michal, David's wife, to Paltiel son of Laish, who was from Gallim.

1. *The name Nabal means "fool." How is Nabal a fool? Is it foolish to hold on to your hard-earned goods and not share them with strangers? Shouldn't we look out for ourselves and our families first?*

2. *Is David right to be angry at Nabal? If he had killed Nabal, would David have still been a man after God's own heart?*

3. *How can we make others less angry at us? At our husbands or wives? What did Abigail do?*

DAY TWO READING AND QUESTIONS

The Ziphites went to Saul at Gibeah and said, "Is not David hiding on the hill of Hakilah, which faces Jeshimon?"

So Saul went down to the Desert of Ziph, with his three thousand select Israelite troops, to search there for David. Saul made his camp beside the road on the hill of Hakilah facing Jeshimon, but David stayed in the wilderness. When he saw that Saul had followed him there, he sent out scouts and learned that Saul had definitely arrived.

Then David set out and went to the place where Saul had camped. He saw where Saul and Abner son of Ner, the commander of the army, had lain down. Saul was lying inside the camp, with the army encamped around him.

David then asked Ahimelek the Hittite and Abishai son of Zeruiah, Joab's brother, "Who will go down into the camp with me to Saul?"

"I'll go with you," said Abishai.

So David and Abishai went to the army by night, and there was Saul, lying asleep inside the camp with his spear stuck in the ground near his head. Abner and the soldiers were lying around him.

Abishai said to David, "Today God has delivered your enemy into your hands. Now let me pin him to the ground with one thrust of the spear; I won't strike him twice."

But David said to Abishai, "Don't destroy him! Who can lay a hand on the LORD's anointed and be guiltless? As surely as the LORD lives," he said, "the LORD himself will strike him, or his time will come and he will die, or he will go into battle and perish. But the LORD forbid that I should lay a hand on the LORD's anointed. Now get the spear and water jug that are near his head, and let's go."

So David took the spear and water jug near Saul's head, and they left. No one saw or knew about it, nor did anyone wake up. They were all sleeping, because the LORD had put them into a deep sleep.

Then David crossed over to the other side and stood on top of the hill some distance away; there was a wide space between them. He called out to the army and to Abner son of Ner, "Aren't you going to answer me, Abner?"

Abner replied, "Who are you who calls to the king?"

David said, "You're a man, aren't you? And who is like you in Israel? Why didn't you guard your lord the king? Someone came to destroy your lord the king. What you have done is not good. As surely as the LORD lives, you and your men must die, because you did not guard your master, the LORD's anointed. Look around you. Where are the king's spear and water jug that were near his head?"

Saul recognized David's voice and said, "Is that your voice, David my son?"

David replied, "Yes it is, my lord the king." And he added, "Why is my lord pursuing his servant? What have I done, and what wrong am I guilty of? Now let my lord the king listen to his servant's words. If the LORD has incited you against me, then may he accept an offering. If, however, people have done it, may they be cursed before the LORD! They have driven me today from my share in the LORD's inheritance and have said, 'Go, serve other gods.' Now do not let my blood fall to the ground far from the presence of the LORD. The king of Israel has come out to look for a flea—as one hunts a partridge in the mountains."

Then Saul said, "I have sinned. Come back, David my son. Because you considered my life precious today, I will not try to harm you again. Surely I have acted like a fool and have been terribly wrong."

"Here is the king's spear," David answered. "Let one of your young men come over and get it. The LORD rewards everyone for their righteousness and faithfulness. The LORD delivered you into my hands today, but I would not lay a hand on the LORD's anointed. As surely as I valued your life today, so may the LORD value my life and deliver me from all trouble."

Then Saul said to David, "May you be blessed, David my son; you will do great things and surely triumph."

So David went on his way, and Saul returned home.

1. *Saul will not leave David alone. Do we sometimes hold on to grudges? What must we do to let go of them?*

2. *Is Saul sincere in his confession of sin for pursuing David? Why doesn't he stop?*

3. *What is the relationship between confession and changing our behavior?*

DAY THREE READING AND QUESTIONS

The Philistines assembled and came and set up camp at Shunem, while Saul gathered all Israel and set up camp at Gilboa. When Saul saw the Philistine army, he was afraid; terror filled his heart. He inquired of the LORD, but the LORD did not answer him by dreams or Urim or prophets. Saul then said to his attendants,

"Find me a woman who is a medium, so I may go and inquire of her."

"There is one in Endor," they said.

So Saul disguised himself, putting on other clothes, and at night he and two men went to the woman. "Consult a spirit for me," he said, "and bring up for me the one I name."

But the woman said to him, "Surely you know what Saul has done. He has cut off the mediums and spiritists from the land. Why have you set a trap for my life to bring about my death?"

Saul swore to her by the LORD, "As surely as the LORD lives, you will not be punished for this."

Then the woman asked, "Whom shall I bring up for you?"

"Bring up Samuel," he said.

When the woman saw Samuel, she cried out at the top of her voice and said to Saul, "Why have you deceived me? You are Saul!"

The king said to her, "Don't be afraid. What do you see?"

The woman said, "I see a ghostly figure coming up out of the earth."

"What does he look like?" he asked.

"An old man wearing a robe is coming up," she said.

Then Saul knew it was Samuel, and he bowed down and prostrated himself with his face to the ground.

Samuel said to Saul, "Why have you disturbed me by bringing me up?"

"I am in great distress," Saul said. "The Philistines are fighting against me, and God has departed from me. He no longer answers me, either by prophets or by dreams. So I have called on you to tell me what to do."

Samuel said, "Why do you consult me, now that the LORD has departed from you and become your enemy? The LORD has done what he predicted through me. The LORD has torn the kingdom out of your hands and given it to one of your neighbors—to David. Because you did not obey the Lord or carry out his fierce wrath against the Amalekites, the Lord has done this to you today. The Lord will deliver both Israel and you into the hands of the Philistines, and tomorrow you and your sons will be with me. The Lord will also give the army of Israel into the hands of the Philistines."

Immediately Saul fell full length on the ground, filled with fear because of Samuel's words. His strength was gone, for he had eaten nothing all that day and all that night.

1. *Can mediums actually recall the spirits of the dead? If so, should we communicate with the dead? Why would we want to?*

2. *What does Saul's desire to see Samuel say about his relationship to God?*

3. *Like Saul, are we willing to listen to God only when we need him? Do we want him to answer us on our own terms? Are we willing to do what it takes to hear God? What does it take?*

DAY FOUR READING AND QUESTIONS

So David and his men got up early in the morning to go back to the land of the Philistines, and the Philistines went up to Jezreel.

David and his men reached Ziklag on the third day. Now the Amalekites had raided the Negev and Ziklag. They had attacked Ziklag and burned it, and had taken captive the women and everyone else in it, both young and old. They killed none of them, but carried them off as they went on their way.

When David and his men reached Ziklag, they found it destroyed by fire and their wives and sons and daughters taken captive. So David and his men wept aloud until they had no strength left to weep. David's two wives had been captured—Ahinoam of Jezreel and Abigail, the widow of Nabal of Carmel. David was greatly distressed because the men were talking of stoning him; each one was bitter in spirit because of his sons and daughters. But David found strength in the LORD his God.

Then David said to Abiathar the priest, the son of Ahimelek, "Bring me the ephod." Abiathar brought it to him, and David inquired of the LORD, "Shall I pursue this raiding party? Will I overtake them?"

"Pursue them," he answered. "You will certainly overtake them and succeed in the rescue."

David and the six hundred men with him came to the Besor Valley, where some stayed behind. Two hundred of them were too exhausted to cross the valley, but David and the other four hundred continued the pursuit.

They found an Egyptian in a field and brought him to David. They gave him water to drink and food to eat—part of a cake of pressed figs and two cakes of raisins. He ate and was revived, for he had not eaten any food or drunk any water for three days and three nights.

David asked him, "Who do you belong to? Where do you come from?"

He said, "I am an Egyptian, the slave of an Amalekite. My master abandoned me when I became ill three days ago. We raided the Negev of the Kerethites, some territory belonging to Judah and the Negev of Caleb. And we burned Ziklag."

David asked him, "Can you lead me down to this raiding party?"

He answered, "Swear to me before God that you will not kill me or hand me over to my master, and I will take you down to them."

He led David down, and there they were, scattered over the countryside, eating, drinking and reveling because of the great amount of plunder they had taken from the land of the Philistines and from Judah. David fought them from dusk until the evening of the next day, and none of them got away, except four hundred young men who rode off on camels and fled. David recovered everything the Amalekites had taken, including his two wives. Nothing was missing: young or old, boy or girl, plunder or anything else they had taken. David brought everything back. He took all the flocks and herds, and his men drove them ahead of the other livestock, saying, "This is David's plunder."

Then David came to the two hundred men who had been too exhausted to follow him and who were left behind at the Besor Valley. They came out to meet David and the men with him. As David and his men approached, he asked them how they were. But all the evil men and troublemakers among David's followers said, "Because they did not go out with us, we will not share with them the plunder we recovered. However, each man may take his wife and children and go."

David replied, "No, my brothers, you must not do that with what the LORD has given us. He has protected us and delivered into our hands the raiding party that came against us. Who will listen to what you say? The share of the man who stayed with the supplies is to be the same as that of him who went down to the battle. All will share alike." David made this a statute and ordinance for Israel from that day to this.

1. *God's command to Saul to completely wipe out the Amalekites may seem harsh to us, but here again they cause harm to God's people. Do*

we trust God's judgment even when we do not understand it? Do we really believe God knows what is best? Or do we sit in judgment against God?

2. *Is it fair for David to give the fruits of battle to those who did not fight? How does David display a heart like God's in this action?*

3. *Is God fair or gracious? Do we get what we deserve from God? Do we give others what they deserve?*

DAY FIVE READING AND QUESTIONS

Now the Philistines fought against Israel; the Israelites fled before them, and many fell dead on Mount Gilboa. The Philistines were in hot pursuit of Saul and his sons, and they killed his sons Jonathan, Abinadab and Malki-Shua. The fighting grew fierce around Saul, and when the archers overtook him, they wounded him critically.

Saul said to his armor-bearer, "Draw your sword and run me through, or these uncircumcised fellows will come and run me through and abuse me."

But his armor-bearer was terrified and would not do it; so Saul took his own sword and fell on it. When the armor-bearer saw that Saul was dead, he too fell on his sword and died with him. So Saul and his three sons and his armor-bearer and all his men died together that same day.

When the Israelites along the valley and those across the Jordan saw that the Israelite army had fled and that Saul and his sons had died, they abandoned their towns and fled. And the Philistines came and occupied them.

The next day, when the Philistines came to strip the dead, they found Saul and his three sons fallen on Mount Gilboa. They cut off his head and stripped off his armor, and they sent messengers throughout the land of the Philistines to proclaim the news in the temple of their idols and among their people. They put his armor in the temple of the Ashtoreths and fastened his body to the wall of Beth Shan.

When the people of Jabesh Gilead heard what the Philistines had done to Saul, all their valiant men marched through the night to Beth Shan. They took down the bodies of Saul and his sons from the wall of Beth Shan and went to Jabesh, where they burned them. Then they took their bones and buried them under a tamarisk tree at Jabesh, and they fasted seven days.

1. *Is Saul right to take his own life? Is this another sign of Saul's fear? Or is he rightly concerned for the dignity of his position as king?*

2. *Were the men of Jabesh Gilead right to give Saul and his sons proper burial? Were they approving Saul's decisions by doing so or simply showing respect for his office as king? Can we know our political leaders are scoundrels and still respect their authority?*

3. *David and Saul face hardships. What are the different attitudes and actions they show in the face of those hardships? How should we face dangers and disasters?*

Meditation on 1 Samuel 25:1–26:25; 28:4–20; 29:11–30:25; 31:1–13

Saul, terrified at the sight of the Philistine army, urgently wants to hear a word from the Lord, but the Lord will not answer him. Why not? Is God a faithless, unreliable God? No. His mercy endures forever. Saul gets no reply from God because Saul will not do what it takes to listen. He will not repent, humble himself, and obey.

But Saul is so desperate to have God on his side (but on Saul's own terms) that he does the unthinkable. Violating the Lord's own law, which Saul himself had previously enforced, Saul goes to a medium and has her call up the spirit of Samuel from the dead. Samuel's news for Saul is not good. God has become Saul's enemy, taken the kingdom from him, and given defeat to Israel in the next day's battle. What's more, Saul and his sons will be dead like Samuel the next day.

Saul faints at the news but is revived by the meal prepared for him by the medium. This proves to be his last meal, like that of a condemned prisoner. He leaves that place and goes to meet his just punishment.

It is frightening to think of being on our own without a word from God. Why would God stop speaking to us? Has he stopped loving us? Does he not care?

No. The love of God is dependable. He is a faithful God who never stops calling on his children with his loving voice. But what if his children refuse to listen? What if God whispers, shouts, even begs us to hear him and we will not? In this section, Saul has so consistently ignored the voice of God that even when Saul thinks he wants to hear God, God will not speak with him. How awful to be deaf to God's voice.

"God who speaks, give us ears to hear you and obey."

MEDITATIONS

2 SAMUEL

A GOD WHO REPAYS THE EVILDOER

1:1–27; 2:8–28; 3:6–15, 17–27; 4:5–5:5 NLT

DAY ONE READING AND QUESTIONS

After the death of Saul, David returned from his victory over the Amalekites and spent two days in Ziklag. On the third day a man arrived from Saul's army camp. He had torn his clothes and put dirt on his head to show that he was in mourning. He fell to the ground before David in deep respect.

"Where have you come from?" David asked.

"I escaped from the Israelite camp," the man replied.

"What happened?" David demanded. "Tell me how the battle went."

The man replied, "Our entire army fled from the battle. Many of the men are dead, and Saul and his son Jonathan are also dead."

"How do you know Saul and Jonathan are dead?" David demanded of the young man.

The man answered, "I happened to be on Mount Gilboa, and there was Saul leaning on his spear with the enemy chariots and charioteers closing in on him. When he turned and saw me, he cried out for me to come to him. 'How can I help?' I asked him.

"He responded, 'Who are you?'

"'I am an Amalekite,' I told him.

"Then he begged me, 'Come over here and put me out of my misery, for I am in terrible pain and want to die.'

"So I killed him," the Amalekite told David, "for I knew he couldn't live. Then I took his crown and his armband, and I have brought them here to you, my lord."

David and his men tore their clothes in sorrow when they heard the news. They mourned and wept and fasted all day for Saul and his son Jonathan, and for the LORD's army and the nation of Israel, because they had died by the sword that day.

Then David said to the young man who had brought the news, "Where are you from?"

And he replied, "I am a foreigner, an Amalekite, who lives in your land."

"Why were you not afraid to kill the LORD's anointed one?" David asked.

Then David said to one of his men, "Kill him!" So the man thrust his sword into the Amalekite and killed him. "You have condemned yourself," David said, "for you yourself confessed that you killed the LORD's anointed one."

1. *Why did the Amalekite claim to have killed Saul? Could he have done this out of mercy and compassion? If so, was his action right? What is wrong with mercy killing?*

2. *Was it God's will that Saul die? If so, was it God's will that David execute the Amalekite? How can that be if God himself had rejected Saul and caused his death?*

3. *Can God work his will through immoral acts? Does that mean God approves those actions?*

DAY TWO READING AND QUESTIONS

Then David composed a funeral song for Saul and Jonathan, and he commanded that it be taught to the people of Judah. It is known as the Song of the Bow, and it is recorded in *The Book of Jashar*.

> Your pride and joy, O Israel, lies dead on the hills!
>   Oh, how the mighty heroes have fallen!
> Don't announce the news in Gath,
>   don't proclaim it in the streets of Ashkelon,
> or the daughters of the Philistines will rejoice
>   and the pagans will laugh in triumph.
>
> O mountains of Gilboa,
>   let there be no dew or rain upon you,
>   nor fruitful fields producing offerings of grain.
> For there the shield of the mighty heroes was defiled;
>   the shield of Saul will no longer be anointed with oil.
> The bow of Jonathan was powerful,
>   and the sword of Saul did its mighty work.
> They shed the blood of their enemies
>   and pierced the bodies of mighty heroes.
>
> How beloved and gracious were Saul and Jonathan!
>   They were together in life and in death.
> They were swifter than eagles,
>   stronger than lions.
> O women of Israel, weep for Saul,
> for he dressed you in luxurious scarlet clothing,
>   in garments decorated with gold.
>
> Oh, how the mighty heroes have fallen in battle!
>   Jonathan lies dead on the hills.
> How I weep for you, my brother Jonathan!
>   Oh, how much I loved you!
> And your love for me was deep,
>   deeper than the love of women!

Oh, how the mighty heroes have fallen!
Stripped of their weapons, they lie dead.

1. *After all David had suffered from Saul, he does not gloat over his death. Why not? Is he honest about Saul or simply refusing to speak evil of the dead? Does his reaction show him to be one after God's own heart?*

2. *We can all relate to the loss of a friend. If you were to write a lament over a dead friend, what would you say? How would you praise them?*

3. *Does lament help grief or preserve it?*

DAY THREE READING AND QUESTIONS

But Abner son of Ner, the commander of Saul's army, had already gone to Mahanaim with Saul's son Ishbosheth. There he proclaimed Ishbosheth king over Gilead, Jezreel, Ephraim, Benjamin, the land of the Ashurites, and all the rest of Israel.

Ishbosheth, Saul's son, was forty years old when he became king, and he ruled from Mahanaim for two years. Meanwhile, the people of Judah remained loyal to David. David made Hebron his capital, and he ruled as king of Judah for seven and a half years.

One day Abner led Ishbosheth's troops from Mahanaim to Gibeon. About the same time, Joab son of Zeruiah led David's troops out and met them at the pool of Gibeon. The two groups sat down there, facing each other from opposite sides of the pool.

Then Abner suggested to Joab, "Let's have a few of our warriors fight hand to hand here in front of us."

"All right," Joab agreed. So twelve men were chosen to fight from each side—twelve men of Benjamin representing Ishbosheth son of Saul, and twelve representing David. Each one grabbed his opponent by the hair and thrust his sword into the other's side so that all of them died. So this place at Gibeon has been known ever since as the Field of Swords.

A fierce battle followed that day, and Abner and the men of Israel were defeated by the forces of David.

Joab, Abishai, and Asahel—the three sons of Zeruiah—were among David's forces that day. Asahel could run like a gazelle, and he began chasing Abner. He pursued him relentlessly, not stopping for anything. When Abner looked back and saw him coming, he called out, "Is that you, Asahel?"

"Yes, it is," he replied.

"Go fight someone else!" Abner warned. "Take on one of the younger men, and strip him of his weapons." But Asahel kept right on chasing Abner.

Again Abner shouted to him, "Get away from here! I don't want to kill you. How could I ever face your brother Joab again?"

But Asahel refused to turn back, so Abner thrust the butt end of his spear through Asahel's stomach, and the spear came out through his back. He stumbled to the ground and died there. And everyone who came by that spot stopped and stood still when they saw Asahel lying there.

When Joab and Abishai found out what had happened, they set out after Abner. The sun was just going down as they arrived at the hill of Ammah near Giah, along the road to the wilderness of Gibeon. Abner's troops from the tribe of Benjamin regrouped there at the top of the hill to take a stand.

Abner shouted down to Joab, "Must we always be killing each other? Don't you realize that bitterness is the only result? When will you call off your men from chasing their Israelite brothers?"

Then Joab said, "God only knows what would have happened if you hadn't spoken, for we would have chased you all night if necessary." So Joab blew the ram's horn, and his men stopped chasing the troops of Israel.

1. *Is Abner guilty for Asahel's death? Did he not warn him? Why did he not want to kill him?*

2. *War among God's people is particularly distasteful. What do you think was God's view of this war?*

3. *What about church fights today? Do they seem particularly bitter because we are God's people? How can we avoid them?*

DAY FOUR READING AND QUESTIONS

As the war between the house of Saul and the house of David went on, Abner became a powerful leader among those loyal to Saul. One day Ishbosheth, Saul's son, accused Abner of sleeping with one of his father's concubines, a woman named Rizpah, daughter of Aiah.

Abner was furious. "Am I some Judean dog to be kicked around like this?" he shouted. "After all I have done for your father, Saul, and his family and friends by not handing you over to David, is this my reward—that you find fault with me about this woman? May God strike me and even kill me if I don't do everything I can to help David get what the LORD has promised him! I'm going to take Saul's kingdom and give it to David. I will establish the throne of David over Israel as well as Judah, all the way from Dan in the north to Beersheba in the south." Ishbosheth didn't dare say another word because he was afraid of what Abner might do.

Then Abner sent messengers to David, saying, "Doesn't the entire land belong to you? Make a solemn pact with me, and I will help turn over all of Israel to you."

"All right," David replied, "but I will not negotiate with you unless you bring back my wife Michal, Saul's daughter, when you come."

David then sent this message to Ishbosheth, Saul's son: "Give me back my wife Michal, for I bought her with the lives of 100 Philistines."

So Ishbosheth took Michal away from her husband, Palti son of Laish. . . .

Meanwhile, Abner had consulted with the elders of Israel. "For some time now," he told them, "you have wanted to make David your king. Now is the time! For the LORD has said, 'I have chosen David to save my people Israel from the hands of the Philistines and from all their other enemies.'" Abner also spoke with the men of Benjamin. Then he went to Hebron to tell David that all the people of Israel and Benjamin had agreed to support him.

When Abner and twenty of his men came to Hebron, David entertained them with a great feast. Then Abner said to David, "Let me go and call an assembly of all Israel to support my lord the king. They will make a covenant with you to make you their king, and you will rule over everything your heart desires." So David sent Abner safely on his way.

But just after David had sent Abner away in safety, Joab and some of David's troops returned from a raid, bringing much plunder with them. When Joab arrived, he was told that Abner had just been there visiting the king and had been sent away in safety.

Joab rushed to the king and demanded, "What have you done? What do you mean by letting Abner get away? You know perfectly well that he came to spy on you and find out everything you're doing!"

Joab then left David and sent messengers to catch up with Abner, asking him to return. They found him at the well of Sirah and brought him back, though David knew nothing about it. When Abner arrived back at Hebron, Joab took him aside at the gateway as if to speak with him privately. But then he stabbed Abner in the stomach and killed him in revenge for killing his brother Asahel. . . .

One day Recab and Baanah, the sons of Rimmon from Beeroth, went to Ishbosheth's house around noon as he was taking his midday rest. The doorkeeper, who had been sifting wheat, became drowsy and fell asleep. So Recab and Baanah slipped past her. They went into the house and found Ishbosheth sleeping on his bed. They struck and killed him and cut off his head. Then, taking his head with them, they fled across the Jordan Valley through the night. When they arrived at Hebron, they presented Ishbosheth's head to David. "Look!" they exclaimed to the king. "Here is the head of Ishbosheth, the son of your enemy Saul who tried to kill you. Today the LORD has given my lord the king revenge on Saul and his entire family!"

But David said to Recab and Baanah, "The LORD, who saves me from all my enemies, is my witness. Someone once told me, 'Saul is dead,' thinking he was bringing me good news. But I seized him and killed him at Ziklag. That's the reward I gave him for his news! How much more should I reward evil men who have killed an innocent man in his own house and on his own bed? Shouldn't I hold you responsible for his blood and rid the earth of you?"

So David ordered his young men to kill them, and they did. They cut off their hands and feet and hung their bodies beside the pool in Hebron. Then they took Ishbosheth's head and buried it in Abner's tomb in Hebron.

Then all the tribes of Israel went to David at Hebron and told him, "We are your own flesh and blood. In the past, when Saul was our king, you were the one who really led the forces of Israel. And the LORD told you, 'You will be the shepherd of my people Israel. You will be Israel's leader.'"

So there at Hebron, King David made a covenant before the LORD with all the elders of Israel. And they anointed him king of Israel.

David was thirty years old when he began to reign, and he reigned forty years in all. He had reigned over Judah from Hebron for seven years and six months, and from Jerusalem he reigned over all Israel and Judah for thirty-three years.

1. *Why did Abner support Ishbosheth? Why did he turn against him?*

2. *Is Abner a man of integrity or an opportunist? Should one be loyal even to a bad cause?*

3. *Is Joab justified in taking revenge on Abner? Why doesn't David dismiss Joab from leading his army? Does politics (and war) make strange bedfellows? Should David align himself with the unrighteous Joab?*

DAY FIVE READING AND QUESTIONS

Go back and read 2 Samuel 1:1–27; 2:8–28; 3:6–15, 17–27; 4:5–5:5.

1. *Is God at work in the actions of Recab and Baanah? Does God cause evil actions, or does he use them to work his will? How does this relate to the story of Judas (see Acts 1:15–20)?*

2. *Sometimes God directly fights for Israel with thunder and a tree-top army. At other times, he works through Saul, David, and other military leaders. Does God work directly at times today, or does he only work through others? How can we know God is fighting our battles?*

3. *David repeatedly shows compassion for his enemies. Is this how he reflects the heart of God? How does God act toward his enemies (see Rom. 5:10)? How should we act toward our enemies (see Matt. 5:43–48; Rom. 12:20)?*

Meditation on 2 Samuel 1:1–27; 2:8–28; 3:6–15, 17–27; 4:5–5:5

After Saul's death, Abner, the commander of Saul's army, makes Ishbosheth, the son of Saul, king of Israel. Meanwhile, the tribe of Judah follows David. Thus begins a civil war in Israel. The first battle of the war occurs at the pool of Gibeon, beginning with a contest between twelve soldiers from each side. The contest is a draw, since all twenty-four die.

One episode in the fierce battle that follows involves Asahel, the brother of Joab and Abishai, who pursues Abner. Abner repeatedly warns Asahel to stop his pursuit, but when he will not, Abner thrusts the butt end of his spear through Asahel, killing him instantly. Joab and Abashai then pursue Abner, who rallies his men behind him on a hill. At that point Abner calls for a truce, asking Joab and David's men to stop their pursuit. They do, and the battle ends—the victory belonging to David's forces who lost nineteen men but killed three hundred and sixty of Abner's men. In this bloody civil war, David's forces grow stronger and stronger.

Civil war. Can there be anything more horrible than brother killing brother? After Saul's death, there is war between the forces of Ishbosheth, the son of Saul, and the forces of David. With this war come deceit, betrayal, and revenge. Where is the voice of God in all this mayhem? Has God abandoned his people? No. He is a faithful God who still speaks and guides those like David who seek to hear him even in the middle of bloodshed and battle.

"Faithful God, when we are surrounded by horrors we do not understand, may we trust you to deliver us from evil."

A GOD WHO KEEPS PROMISES

6:1–7:17; 8:1–6; 8:13–9:13 NIV

DAY ONE READING AND QUESTIONS

David again brought together all the able young men of Israel—thirty thousand. He and all his men went to Baalah in Judah to bring up from there the ark of God, which is called by the Name, the name of the LORD Almighty, who is enthroned between the cherubim on the ark. They set the ark of God on a new cart and brought it from the house of Abinadab, which was on the hill. Uzzah and Ahio, sons of Abinadab, were guiding the new cart with the ark of God on it, and Ahio was walking in front of it. David and all Israel were celebrating with all their might before the LORD, with castanets, harps, lyres, timbrels, sistrums and cymbals.

When they came to the threshing floor of Nakon, Uzzah reached out and took hold of the ark of God, because the oxen stumbled. The LORD's anger burned against Uzzah because of his irreverent act; therefore God struck him down, and he died there beside the ark of God.

Then David was angry because the LORD's wrath had broken out against Uzzah, and to this day that place is called Perez Uzzah.

David was afraid of the LORD that day and said, "How can the ark of the LORD ever come to me?" He was not willing to take the ark of the LORD to be with him in the City of David. Instead, he took it to the house of Obed-Edom the Gittite.The ark of the LORD remained in the house of Obed-Edom the Gittite for three months, and the LORD blessed him and his entire household.

Now King David was told, "The LORD has blessed the household of Obed-Edom and everything he has, because of the ark of God." So David went to bring up the ark of God from the house of Obed-Edom to the City of David with rejoicing. When those who were carrying the ark of the LORD had taken six steps, he sacrificed a bull and a fattened calf. Wearing a linen ephod, David was dancing before the LORD with all his might, while he and all Israel were bringing up the ark of the LORD with shouts and the sound of trumpets.

As the ark of the LORD was entering the City of David, Michal daughter of Saul watched from a window. And when she saw King David leaping and dancing before the LORD, she despised him in her heart.

They brought the ark of the LORD and set it in its place inside the tent that David had pitched for it, and David sacrificed burnt offerings and fellowship offerings before the LORD. After he had finished sacrificing the burnt offerings and fellowship offerings, he blessed the people in the name of the LORD Almighty. Then he gave a loaf of bread, a cake of dates and a cake of raisins to each person in the whole crowd of Israelites, both men and women. And all the people went to their homes.

When David returned home to bless his household, Michal daughter of Saul came out to meet him and said, "How the king of Israel has distinguished himself today, going around half-naked in full view of the slave girls of his servants as any vulgar fellow would!"

David said to Michal, "It was before the LORD, who chose me rather than your father or anyone from his house when he appointed me ruler over the LORD's people Israel—I will celebrate before the LORD. I will become even more undignified than this, and I will be humiliated in my own eyes. But by these slave girls you spoke of, I will be held in honor."

And Michal daughter of Saul had no children to the day of her death.

1. *Was Uzzah right to try and save the ark from falling? Was his heart right before God? Is God's punishment of him harsh? What lesson about God can we learn from this story?*

2. *Was Michal right to worry about David's dignity as king?*

3. *Should we be joyous and dance before the Lord in worship? Why or why not? Is this dignified? Should we be concerned about what others think of our worship?*

DAY TWO READING AND QUESTIONS

After the king was settled in his palace and the LORD had given him rest from all his enemies around him, he said to Nathan the prophet, "Here I am, living in a house of cedar, while the ark of God remains in a tent."

Nathan replied to the king, "Whatever you have in mind, go ahead and do it, for the LORD is with you."

But that night the word of the LORD came to Nathan, saying:

"Go and tell my servant David, 'This is what the LORD says: Are you the one to build me a house to dwell in? I have not dwelt in a house from the day I brought the Israelites up out of Egypt to this day. I have been moving from place to place with a tent as my dwelling. Wherever I have moved with all the Israelites, did I ever say to any of their rulers whom I commanded to shepherd my people Israel, "Why have you not built me a house of cedar?"'

"Now then, tell my servant David, 'This is what the LORD Almighty says: I took you from the pasture, from tending the flock, and appointed you ruler over my people Israel. I have been with you wherever you have gone, and I have cut off all your enemies from before you. Now I will make your name great, like the names of the greatest men on earth. And I will provide a place for my people Israel and will plant them so that they can have a home of their own and no longer be disturbed. Wicked people will not oppress them anymore, as they did at the beginning and have done ever since the time I appointed leaders over my people Israel. I will also give you rest from all your enemies.

"'The LORD declares to you that the LORD himself will establish a house for you: When your days are over and you rest with your ancestors, I will raise up your offspring to succeed you, your own flesh and blood, and I will establish his kingdom. He is the one who will build a house for my Name, and I will establish the throne of his kingdom forever. I will be his father, and he will be my son. When he does wrong, I will punish him with a rod wielded by men, with floggings inflicted by human hands. But my love will never be taken away from him, as I took it away from Saul, whom I removed from before you. Your house and your kingdom will endure forever before me; your throne will be established forever.'"

Nathan reported to David all the words of this entire revelation.

1. *Why doesn't God allow David to build the temple?*

2. *Church buildings are not exactly temples (or tabernacles), but should we be concerned (like David) when our houses are so much better than our church buildings? Read Haggai 1:2–11 before you answer.*

3. *Can we outgive God? How has he surprised you with blessings? What should our response be to his promises?*

DAY THREE READING AND QUESTIONS

In the course of time, David defeated the Philistines and subdued them, and he took Metheg Ammah from the control of the Philistines.

David also defeated the Moabites. He made them lie down on the ground and measured them off with a length of cord. Every two lengths of them were put to death, and the third length was allowed to live. So the Moabites became subject to David and brought him tribute.

Moreover, David defeated Hadadezer son of Rehob, king of Zobah, when he went to restore his monument at the Euphrates River. David captured a thousand of his chariots, seven thousand charioteers and twenty thousand foot soldiers. He hamstrung all but a hundred of the chariot horses.

When the Arameans of Damascus came to help Hadadezer king of Zobah, David struck down twenty-two thousand of them. He put garrisons in the Aramean kingdom of Damascus, and the Arameans became subject to him and brought tribute. The Lord gave David victory wherever he went. . . .

And David became famous after he returned from striking down eighteen thousand Edomites in the Valley of Salt.

He put garrisons throughout Edom, and all the Edomites became subject to David. The LORD gave David victory wherever he went.

David reigned over all Israel, doing what was just and right for all his people. Joab son of Zeruiah was over the army; Jehoshaphat son of Ahilud was recorder; Zadok son of Ahitub and Ahimelek son of Abiathar were priests; Seraiah was secretary; Benaiah son of Jehoiada was over the Kerethites and Pelethites; and David's sons were priests.

1. *When God blesses us with safety from enemies, how should we respond?*

2. *When God gives us wealth, what should we do with it? Do blessings always entail responsibility?*

3. *Should David have made his sons priests? What does this tell us about David? Are the heroes of Scripture sinless? Is David? At this point, is he still a man after God's own heart?*

DAY FOUR READING AND QUESTIONS

David asked, "Is there anyone still left of the house of Saul to whom I can show kindness for Jonathan's sake?"

Now there was a servant of Saul's household named Ziba. They summoned him to appear before David, and the king said to him, "Are you Ziba?"

"At your service," he replied.

The king asked, "Is there no one still alive from the house of Saul to whom I can show God's kindness?"

Ziba answered the king, "There is still a son of Jonathan; he is lame in both feet."

"Where is he?" the king asked.

Ziba answered, "He is at the house of Makir son of Ammiel in Lo Debar."

So King David had him brought from Lo Debar, from the house of Makir son of Ammiel.

When Mephibosheth son of Jonathan, the son of Saul, came to David, he bowed down to pay him honor.

David said, "Mephibosheth!"

"At your service," he replied.

"Don't be afraid," David said to him, "for I will surely show you kindness for the sake of your father Jonathan. I will restore to you all the land that belonged to your grandfather Saul, and you will always eat at my table."

Mephibosheth bowed down and said, "What is your servant, that you should notice a dead dog like me?"

Then the king summoned Ziba, Saul's steward, and said to him, "I have given your master's grandson everything that belonged to Saul and his family. You and your sons and your servants are to farm the land for him and bring in the crops, so that your master's grandson may be provided for. And Mephibosheth, grandson of your master, will always eat at my table." (Now Ziba had fifteen sons and twenty servants.)

Then Ziba said to the king, "Your servant will do whatever my lord the king commands his servant to do." So Mephibosheth ate at David's table like one of the king's sons.

Mephibosheth had a young son named Mika, and all the members of Ziba's household were servants of Mephibosheth. And Mephibosheth lived in Jerusalem, because he always ate at the king's table; he was lame in both feet.

1. *Like God, David keeps his vows and promises. Do we make vows to God today? To others?*

2. *Do we keep those vows even when it is difficult? Aren't all children of God to be promise keepers?*

3. *Showing mercy to a lame man reminds us of Jesus (Matt. 11:5; 15:30–31; 21:14) and the early Christians (Acts 3:2–10; 8:7). Are we to care for the disabled today? How? Why?*

DAY FIVE READING AND QUESTIONS

Go back and read 2 Samuel 6:1–7:17; 8:1–6; 8:13–9:13.

1. *Uzzah's touching of the ark is an irreverent act. David sings and dances before the Lord in what Michal thinks is an undignified manner. What does it mean to be reverent before God? Is being reverent the same as being proper or dignified?*

2. *Would visitors to your church think you were reverent in your worship? Would they think you were joyous? How would they know?*

3. *Like David, do we sometimes want to do something great for God like build him a temple or grow him a church? Isn't being grateful to God the greatest thing we can do? Is this what David learns? How does he show his gratitude? How do we?*

Meditation on 2 Samuel 6:1–7:17; 8:1–6; 8:13–9:13

Once the ark comes to Jerusalem, David is embarrassed that he lives in a palace of cedar while the ark remains in a tent. He therefore offers to build a house, a temple, for God.

God's response to David's offer is surprising. Instead of David building a house for the Lord, the Lord promises to build one for David—not a literal house, but a dynasty, "the house of David" (comparable to "the house of Windsor" in England). Before David, there was no dynasty among judges, prophets, or kings, since the sons of Eli, Samuel, and Saul proved a disappointment to God and to the people. By contrast, David will have a son blessed by God who will establish his kingdom.

David responds with a heartfelt prayer of thanksgiving and praise. He knows he does not deserve this great blessing, but he boldly calls on God to keep his promises. He praises God as the one who delivered Israel from bondage in Egypt, the God whose words are trustworthy and powerful, the God whose will rules over all. David knows he has not brought blessings to Israel, but the Lord God who reigns in mercy has showered them with his love.

God has established David's kingdom, given him victory over his enemies, and granted him a new capital, Jerusalem. What more can David ask? He asks for nothing more, but God promises more—he will make the name of David great and establish the kingdom of his son forever. He truly is the God who can do "immeasurably more than all we ask or imagine" (Eph. 3:20 NIV). David in turn takes the blessings of the Lord and shares them with those in need, such as the lame Mephibosheth. When God keeps his promises to us, we must share his bounty with others.

"God of blessing, may we show our gratitude by being a blessing to others."

A GOD WHO TAKES AWAY SIN

10:1–11:17; 11:22–12:25 NLT

DAY ONE READING AND QUESTIONS

Some time after this, King Nahash of the Ammonites died, and his son Hanun became king. David said, "I am going to show loyalty to Hanun just as his father, Nahash, was always loyal to me." So David sent ambassadors to express sympathy to Hanun about his father's death.

But when David's ambassadors arrived in the land of Ammon, the Ammonite commanders said to Hanun, their master, "Do you really think these men are coming here to honor your father? No! David has sent them to spy out the city so they can come in and conquer it!" So Hanun seized David's ambassadors and shaved off half of each man's beard, cut off their robes at the buttocks, and sent them back to David in shame.

When David heard what had happened, he sent messengers to tell the men, "Stay at Jericho until your beards grow out, and then come back." For they felt deep shame because of their appearance.

When the people of Ammon realized how seriously they had angered David, they sent and hired 20,000 Aramean foot soldiers from the lands of Beth-rehob and Zobah, 1,000 from the king of Maacah, and 12,000 from the land of Tob. When David heard about this, he sent Joab and all his warriors to fight them. The Ammonite troops came out and drew up their battle lines at the entrance of the city gate, while the Arameans from Zobah and Rehob and the men from Tob and Maacah positioned themselves to fight in the open fields.

When Joab saw that he would have to fight on both the front and the rear, he chose some of Israel's elite troops and placed them under his personal command to fight the Arameans in the fields. He left the rest of the army under the command of his brother Abishai, who was to attack the Ammonites. "If the Arameans are too strong for me, then come over and help me," Joab told his brother. "And if the Ammonites are too strong for you, I will come and help you. Be courageous! Let us fight bravely for our people and the cities of our God. May the LORD's will be done."

When Joab and his troops attacked, the Arameans began to run away. And when the Ammonites saw the Arameans running, they ran from Abishai and retreated into the city. After the battle was over, Joab returned to Jerusalem.

The Arameans now realized that they were no match for Israel. So when they regrouped, they were joined by additional Aramean troops summoned by Hadadezer from the other side of the Euphrates River. These troops arrived at Helam under the command of Shobach, the commander of Hadadezer's forces.

When David heard what was happening, he mobilized all Israel, crossed the Jordan River, and led the army to Helam. The Arameans positioned themselves in battle formation and fought against David. But again the Arameans fled from the Israelites. This time David's forces killed 700 charioteers and 40,000 foot soldiers, including Shobach, the commander of their army. When all the kings allied with Hadadezer saw that they had been defeated by Israel, they surrendered to Israel and became their subjects. After that, the Arameans were afraid to help the Ammonites.

1. *Hanun does not just attack Israel, he humiliates their delegates. What is harder to forgive, direct attack or subtle humiliation?*

2. *When was the last time someone embarrassed or humiliated you? What was your reaction? How did Jesus react to shame?*

3. *David tries to be kind to Hanun, but his kindness is repaid with distrust. Have you ever tried to help someone only to have them turn on you? How did you react? How should we treat those who hurt us even when we are trying to help them?*

DAY TWO READING AND QUESTIONS

In the spring of the year, when kings normally go out to war, David sent Joab and the Israelite army to fight the Ammonites. They destroyed the Ammonite army and laid siege to the city of Rabbah. However, David stayed behind in Jerusalem.

Late one afternoon, after his midday rest, David got out of bed and was walking on the roof of the palace. As he looked out over the city, he noticed a woman of unusual beauty taking a bath. He sent someone to find out who she was, and he was told, "She is Bathsheba, the daughter of Eliam and the wife of Uriah the Hittite." Then David sent messengers to get her; and when she came to the palace, he slept with her. She had just completed the purification rites after having her menstrual period. Then she returned home. Later, when Bathsheba discovered that she was pregnant, she sent David a message, saying, "I'm pregnant."

Then David sent word to Joab: "Send me Uriah the Hittite." So Joab sent him to David. When Uriah arrived, David asked him how Joab and the army were getting along and how the war was progressing. Then he told Uriah, "Go on home and relax." David even sent a gift to Uriah after he had left the palace. But

Uriah didn't go home. He slept that night at the palace entrance with the king's palace guard.

When David heard that Uriah had not gone home, he summoned him and asked, "What's the matter? Why didn't you go home last night after being away for so long?"

Uriah replied, "The Ark and the armies of Israel and Judah are living in tents, and Joab and my master's men are camping in the open fields. How could I go home to wine and dine and sleep with my wife? I swear that I would never do such a thing."

"Well, stay here today," David told him, "and tomorrow you may return to the army." So Uriah stayed in Jerusalem that day and the next. Then David invited him to dinner and got him drunk. But even then he couldn't get Uriah to go home to his wife. Again he slept at the palace entrance with the king's palace guard.

So the next morning David wrote a letter to Joab and gave it to Uriah to deliver. The letter instructed Joab, "Station Uriah on the front lines where the battle is fiercest. Then pull back so that he will be killed." So Joab assigned Uriah to a spot close to the city wall where he knew the enemy's strongest men were fighting. And when the enemy soldiers came out of the city to fight, Uriah the Hittite was killed along with several other Israelite soldiers. . . .

So the messenger went to Jerusalem and gave a complete report to David. "The enemy came out against us in the open fields," he said. "And as we chased them back to the city gate, the archers on the wall shot arrows at us. Some of the king's men were killed, including Uriah the Hittite."

"Well, tell Joab not to be discouraged," David said. "The sword devours this one today and that one tomorrow! Fight harder next time, and conquer the city!"

When Uriah's wife heard that her husband was dead, she mourned for him. When the period of mourning was over, David sent for her and brought her to the palace, and she became one of his wives. Then she gave birth to a son. But the LORD was displeased with what David had done.

1. *What is more threatening to our faith and morality, hardship or ease? Are we more prone to forget God when things are going well? Why? Should we desire bad times to bring us closer to God?*

2. *What is worse, David's adultery sin or his attempt to cover it up? Whom is David trying to deceive?*

3. *Why do we find it so hard to admit specific sins? How do we try to cover up?*

DAY THREE READING AND QUESTIONS

So the LORD sent Nathan the prophet to tell David this story: "There were two men in a certain town. One was rich, and one was poor. The rich man owned a great many sheep and cattle. The poor man owned nothing but one little lamb he had bought. He raised that little lamb, and it grew up with his children. It ate from the man's own plate and drank from his cup. He cuddled it in his arms like a baby daughter. One day a guest arrived at the home of the rich man. But instead of killing an animal from his own flock or herd, he took the poor man's lamb and killed it and prepared it for his guest."

David was furious. "As surely as the LORD lives," he vowed, "any man who would do such a thing deserves to die! He must repay four lambs to the poor man for the one he stole and for having no pity."

Then Nathan said to David, "You are that man! The LORD, the God of Israel, says: I anointed you king of Israel and saved you from the power of Saul. I gave you your master's house and his wives and the kingdoms of Israel and Judah. And if that had not been enough, I would have given you much, much more. Why, then, have you despised the word of the LORD and done this horrible deed? For you have murdered Uriah the Hittite with the sword of the Ammonites and stolen his wife. From this time on, your family will live by the sword because you have despised me by taking Uriah's wife to be your own."

1. *Adultery. Murder. Abuse of the powerless. Which is the worst sin? Which one does Nathan focus on in the story he tells?*

2. *Do we abuse others with our power in less dramatic ways than adultery and murder? How can we use power and influence with compassion?*

3. *Perhaps David's worst sin is ingratitude toward God. Do we sometimes repay God's blessings with disobedience? What is the relationship between gratitude and hearing God?*

DAY FOUR READING AND QUESTIONS

"This is what the LORD says: Because of what you have done, I will cause your own household to rebel against you. I will give your wives to another man before your very eyes, and he will go to bed with them in public view. You did it secretly, but I will make this happen to you openly in the sight of all Israel."

Then David confessed to Nathan, "I have sinned against the LORD."

Nathan replied, "Yes, but the LORD has forgiven you, and you won't die for this sin. Nevertheless, because you have shown utter contempt for the word of the LORD by doing this, your child will die."

After Nathan returned to his home, the LORD sent a deadly illness to the child of David and Uriah's wife. David begged God to spare the child. He went without food and lay all night on the bare ground. The elders of his household pleaded with him to get up and eat with them, but he refused.

Then on the seventh day the child died. David's advisers were afraid to tell him. "He wouldn't listen to reason while the child was ill," they said. "What drastic thing will he do when we tell him the child is dead?"

When David saw them whispering, he realized what had happened. "Is the child dead?" he asked.

"Yes," they replied, "he is dead."

Then David got up from the ground, washed himself, put on lotions, and changed his clothes. He went to the Tabernacle and worshiped the LORD. After that, he returned to the palace and was served food and ate.

His advisers were amazed. "We don't understand you," they told him. "While the child was still living, you wept and refused to eat. But now that the child is dead, you have stopped your mourning and are eating again."

David replied, "I fasted and wept while the child was alive, for I said, 'Perhaps the LORD will be gracious to me and let the child live.' But why should I fast when he is dead? Can I bring him back again? I will go to him one day, but he cannot return to me."

Then David comforted Bathsheba, his wife, and slept with her. She became pregnant and gave birth to a son, and David named him Solomon. The LORD loved the child and sent word through Nathan the prophet that they should name him Jedidiah (which means "beloved of the LORD"), as the LORD had commanded.

1. *David's child dies because of David's sin. Is this fair? Have you suffered because of the sins of others? Do others suffer because of our sins? Does that suffering act as discipline, causing us to be more obedient to God?*

2. *How does God show his mercy in this story? Is God simply an angry God, waiting for us to sin so he can punish us?*

3. *How does God continue to work his will in spite of David's disobedience? In spite of our disobedience?*

DAY FIVE READING AND QUESTIONS

Go back and read 2 Samuel 10:1–11:17; 11:22–12:25.

1. *Read Psalm 51, the psalm of repentance David wrote after Nathan came to him. What phrases from this psalm express genuine remorse? What phrases express confidence in God's forgiveness? What phrases call for changing one's life?*

2. *Do we sometimes put so much trust in Christian leaders that we are utterly shocked when they fall? How should we treat fallen leaders? How does Nathan treat David?*

3. *How does the story of David and Bathsheba show the importance of continuing to listen to God?*

Meditation on 2 Samuel 10:1–11:17; 11:22–12:25

It's one of the saddest stories in the Bible. David, the man after God's own heart, turns his heart away from God by turning his eyes toward Bathsheba. David, who showed mercy to his greatest enemies, now has his most loyal soldier killed. What's hardest to believe is that he does all this with a clear conscience. Only when confronted by the voice of God through a prophet's story does David realize his sin and face the horrible consequences of his actions.

The Lord does not condone David's actions, but neither does he abandon David. The Lord speaks. He sends Nathan the prophet to David with the story of a rich man who abuses a poor man, taking the poor man's one lamb (like a pet to the poor man) to serve as supper for the rich man's guest. David is outraged at the story and says the man deserves death but must pay back four times over for the lamb.

"You are the man," says Nathan. The Lord had blessed David beyond his imagination, making him wealthy and powerful. God would have blessed him even more, but David repaid his blessing by despising the word of the Lord. David, the man after God's own heart, has turned his heart against God, stopped his ears against God's voice, and disobeyed God as heinously as Saul ever did.

But in his mercy, God forgives him. David will not die. But there are consequences to the sin. God punishes and disciplines those whom he loves. The sword will not depart from David's family. One close to David will humiliate him by sleeping with his wives, just as David had done to Uriah. The child Bathsheba carries is condemned to die.

But God does not abandon David. He and Bathsheba have another son, Solomon, who is also known as Jedidiah, "loved by the LORD." The Lord also gives David victory over the Ammonites. David had fallen as low as one can go. God has raised him up.

"God of mercy, we have sinned against you. Forgive us as you forgave David."

A GOD WHO DISCIPLINES THOSE HE LOVES

13:1–16:14 ESV

DAY ONE READING AND QUESTIONS

Now Absalom, David's son, had a beautiful sister, whose name was Tamar. And after a time Amnon, David's son, loved her. And Amnon was so tormented that he made himself ill because of his sister Tamar, for she was a virgin, and it seemed impossible to Amnon to do anything to her. But Amnon had a friend, whose name was Jonadab, the son of Shimeah, David's brother. And Jonadab was a very crafty man. And he said to him, "O son of the king, why are you so haggard morning after morning? Will you not tell me?" Amnon said to him, "I love Tamar, my brother Absalom's sister." Jonadab said to him, "Lie down on your bed and pretend to be ill. And when your father comes to see you, say to him, 'Let my sister Tamar come and give me bread to eat, and prepare the food in my sight, that I may see it and eat it from her hand.'" So Amnon lay down and pretended to be ill. And when the king came to see him, Amnon said to the king, "Please let my sister Tamar come and make a couple of cakes in my sight, that I may eat from her hand."

Then David sent home to Tamar, saying, "Go to your brother Amnon's house and prepare food for him." So Tamar went to her brother Amnon's house, where he was lying down. And she took dough and kneaded it and made cakes in his sight and baked the cakes. And she took the pan and emptied it out before him, but he refused to eat. And Amnon said, "Send out everyone from me." So everyone went out from him. Then Amnon said to Tamar, "Bring the food into the chamber, that I may eat from your hand." And Tamar took the cakes she had made and brought them into the chamber to Amnon her brother. But when she brought them near him to eat, he took hold of her and said to her, "Come, lie with me, my sister." She answered him, "No, my brother, do not violate me, for such a thing is not done in Israel; do not do this outrageous thing. As for me, where could I carry my shame? And as for you, you would be as one of the outrageous fools in Israel. Now therefore, please speak to the king, for he will not withhold me from you." But he would not listen to her, and being stronger than she, he violated her and lay with her.

Then Amnon hated her with very great hatred, so that the hatred with which he hated her was greater than the love with which he had loved her. And Amnon said to her, "Get up! Go!" But she said to him, "No, my brother, for this wrong in sending me away is greater than the other that you did to me." But he would not listen to her. He called the young man who served him and said, "Put this woman out of my presence and bolt the door after her." Now she was wearing a long robe with sleeves, for thus were the virgin daughters of the king dressed. So his servant put her out and bolted the door after her. And Tamar put ashes on her head and tore the long robe that she wore. And she laid her hand on her head and went away, crying aloud as she went.

And her brother Absalom said to her, "Has Amnon your brother been with you? Now hold your peace, my sister. He is your brother; do not take this to heart." So Tamar lived, a desolate woman, in her brother Absalom's house. When King David heard of all these things, he was very angry. But Absalom spoke to Amnon neither good nor bad, for Absalom hated Amnon, because he had violated his sister Tamar.

After two full years Absalom had sheepshearers at Baal-hazor, which is near Ephraim, and Absalom invited all the king's sons. And Absalom came to the king and said, "Behold, your servant has sheepshearers. Please let the king and his servants go with your servant." But the king said to Absalom, "No, my son, let us not all go, lest we be burdensome to you." He pressed him, but he would not go but gave him his blessing. Then Absalom said, "If not, please let my brother Amnon go with us." And the king said to him, "Why should he go with you?" But Absalom pressed him until he let Amnon and all the king's sons go with him. Then Absalom commanded his servants, "Mark when Amnon's heart is merry with wine, and when I say to you, 'Strike Amnon,' then kill him. Do not fear; have I not commanded you? Be courageous and be valiant." So the servants of Absalom did to Amnon as Absalom had commanded. Then all the king's sons arose, and each mounted his mule and fled.

While they were on the way, news came to David, "Absalom has struck down all the king's sons, and not one of them is left." Then the king arose and tore his garments and lay on the earth. And all his servants who were standing by tore their garments. But Jonadab the son of Shimeah, David's brother, said, "Let not my lord suppose that they have killed all the young men, the king's sons, for Amnon alone is dead. For by the command of Absalom this has been determined from the day he violated his sister Tamar. Now therefore let not my lord the king so take it to heart as to suppose that all the king's sons are dead, for Amnon alone is dead."

But Absalom fled. And the young man who kept the watch lifted up his eyes and looked, and behold, many people were coming from the road behind him by the side of the mountain. And Jonadab said to the king, "Behold, the king's sons have come; as your servant said, so it has come about." And as soon as he had finished speaking, behold, the king's sons came and lifted up their voice and wept. And the king also and all his servants wept very bitterly.

But Absalom fled and went to Talmai the son of Ammihud, king of Geshur. And David mourned for his son day after day. So Absalom fled and went to Geshur, and was there three years. And the spirit of the king longed to go out to Absalom, because he was comforted about Amnon, since he was dead.

1. *Is Amnon really in love with Tamar? What is the difference between love and lust? Where had Amnon learned to try to possess by any means a woman he desired? Do children learn more from our words or our examples?*

2. *Where had Absalom learned to be deceitful in causing another's death? Did Absalom repent of his actions?*

3. *Why does David so easily forgive Absalom? Are parents blind to the sins of their favorites?*

DAY TWO READING AND QUESTIONS

Now Joab the son of Zeruiah knew that the king's heart went out to Absalom. And Joab sent to Tekoa and brought from there a wise woman and said to her, "Pretend to be a mourner and put on mourning garments. Do not anoint yourself with oil, but behave like a woman who has been mourning many days for the dead. Go to the king and speak thus to him." So Joab put the words in her mouth.

When the woman of Tekoa came to the king, she fell on her face to the ground and paid homage and said, "Save me, O king."

And the king said to her, "What is your trouble?" She answered, "Alas, I am a widow; my husband is dead. And your servant had two sons, and they quarreled with one another in the field. There was no one to separate them, and one struck the other and killed him. And now the whole clan has risen against your servant, and they say, 'Give up the man who struck his brother, that we may put him to death for the life of his brother whom he killed.' And so they would destroy the heir also. Thus they would quench my coal that is left and leave to my husband neither name nor remnant on the face of the earth."

Then the king said to the woman, "Go to your house, and I will give orders concerning you." And the woman of Tekoa said to the king, "On me be the guilt, my lord the king, and on my father's house; let the king and his throne be guiltless." The king said, "If anyone says anything to you, bring him to me, and he shall never touch you again." Then she said, "Please let the king invoke the LORD your God, that the avenger of blood kill no more, and my son be not destroyed." He said, "As the LORD lives, not one hair of your son shall fall to the ground."

Then the woman said, "Please let your servant speak a word to my lord the king." He said, "Speak." And the woman said, "Why then have you planned such a thing against the people of God? For in giving this decision the king convicts himself, inasmuch as the king does not bring his banished one home again. We must all die; we are like water spilled on the ground, which cannot be gathered up again. But God will not take away life, and he devises means so that the banished one will not remain an outcast. Now I have come to say this to my lord the king because the people have made me afraid, and your servant thought, 'I will speak to the king; it may be that the king will perform the request of his servant. For the king will hear and deliver his servant from the hand of the man who would destroy me and my son together from the heritage of God.' And your servant thought, 'The word of my lord the king will set me at rest,' for my lord the king is like the angel of God to discern good and evil. The LORD your God be with you!"

Then the king answered the woman, "Do not hide from me anything I ask you." And the woman said, "Let my lord the king speak." The king said, "Is the hand of Joab with you in all this?" The woman answered and said, "As surely as you live, my lord the king, one cannot turn to the right hand or to the left from anything that my lord the king has said. It was your servant Joab who commanded me; it was he who put all these words in the mouth of your servant. In order to change the course of things your servant Joab did this. But my lord has wisdom like the wisdom of the angel of God to know all things that are on the earth."

Then the king said to Joab, "Behold now, I grant this; go, bring back the young man Absalom." And Joab fell on his face to the ground and paid homage and blessed the king. And Joab said, "Today your servant knows that I have found favor in your sight, my lord the king, in that the king has granted the request of his servant." So Joab arose and went to Geshur and brought Absalom to Jerusalem. And the king said, "Let him dwell apart in his own house; he is not to come into my presence." So Absalom lived apart in his own house and did not come into the king's presence.

Now in all Israel there was no one so much to be praised for his handsome appearance as Absalom. From the sole of his foot to the crown of his head there was no blemish in him. And when he cut the hair of his head (for at the end of every year he used to cut it; when it was heavy on him, he cut it), he weighed the hair of his head, two hundred shekels by the king's weight.

> There were born to Absalom three sons, and one daughter whose name was Tamar. She was a beautiful woman.
>
> So Absalom lived two full years in Jerusalem, without coming into the king's presence. Then Absalom sent for Joab, to send him to the king, but Joab would not come to him. And he sent a second time, but Joab would not come. Then he said to his servants, "See, Joab's field is next to mine, and he has barley there; go and set it on fire." So Absalom's servants set the field on fire. Then Joab arose and went to Absalom at his house and said to him, "Why have your servants set my field on fire?" Absalom answered Joab, "Behold, I sent word to you, 'Come here, that I may send you to the king, to ask, "Why have I come from Geshur? It would be better for me to be there still." Now therefore let me go into the presence of the king, and if there is guilt in me, let him put me to death.'" Then Joab went to the king and told him, and he summoned Absalom. So he came to the king and bowed himself on his face to the ground before the king, and the king kissed Absalom.

1. *Why do stories sometimes move our hearts in ways that mere instruction does not? What about the woman's story moved David? What about it moves you?*

2. *The woman says God devises ways to give life and restore the banished (14:14). In light of that, is David right to restore Absalom? Is he again displaying the heart of God?*

3. *On the other hand, was this restoration foolish on David's part? Under what circumstances should we receive sinners back?*

DAY THREE READING AND QUESTIONS

After this Absalom got himself a chariot and horses, and fifty men to run before him. And Absalom used to rise early and stand beside the way of the gate. And when any man had a dispute to come before the king for judgment, Absalom would call to him and say, "From what city are you?" And when he said, "Your servant is of such and such a tribe in Israel," Absalom would say to him, "See, your claims are good and right, but there is no man designated by the king to hear you." Then Absalom would say, "Oh that I were judge in the land! Then every man with a dispute or cause might come to me, and I would give him justice." And whenever a man came near to pay homage to him, he would put out his hand and take hold of him and kiss him. Thus Absalom did to all of Israel who came to the king for judgment. So Absalom stole the hearts of the men of Israel.

And at the end of four years Absalom said to the king, "Please let me go and pay my vow, which I have vowed to the LORD, in Hebron. For your servant vowed a vow while I lived at Geshur in Aram, saying, 'If the LORD will indeed bring me back to Jerusalem, then I will offer worship to the LORD.'" The king said to him, "Go in peace." So he arose and went to Hebron. But Absalom sent secret messengers throughout all the tribes of Israel, saying, "As soon as you hear the sound of the trumpet, then say, 'Absalom is king at Hebron!'" With Absalom went two hundred men from Jerusalem who were invited guests, and they went in their innocence and knew nothing. And while Absalom was offering the sacrifices, he sent for Ahithophel the Gilonite, David's counselor, from his city Giloh. And the conspiracy grew strong, and the people with Absalom kept increasing.

And a messenger came to David, saying, "The hearts of the men of Israel have gone after Absalom." Then David said to all his servants who were with him at Jerusalem, "Arise, and let us flee, or else there will be no escape for us from Absalom. Go quickly, lest he overtake us quickly and bring down ruin on us and strike the city with the edge of the sword." And the king's servants said to the king, "Behold, your servants are ready to do whatever my lord the king decides." So the king went out, and all his household after him. And the king left ten concubines to keep the house. And the king went out, and all the people after him. And they halted at the last house.

And all his servants passed by him, and all the Cherethites, and all the Pelethites, and all the six hundred Gittites who had followed him from Gath, passed on before the king. Then the king said to Ittai the Gittite, "Why do you also go with us? Go back and stay with the king, for you are a foreigner and also an exile from your home. You came only yesterday, and shall I today make you wander about with us, since I go I know not where? Go back and take your brothers with you, and may the LORD show steadfast love and faithfulness to you." But Ittai answered the king, "As the LORD lives, and as my lord the king lives, wherever my lord the king shall be, whether for death or for life, there also will your servant be." And David said to Ittai, "Go then, pass on." So Ittai the Gittite passed on with all his men and all the little ones who were with him. And all the land wept aloud as all the people passed by, and the king crossed the brook Kidron, and all the people passed on toward the wilderness.

And Abiathar came up, and behold, Zadok came also with all the Levites, bearing the ark of the covenant of God. And they set down the ark of God until the people had all passed out of the city. Then the king said to Zadok, "Carry the ark of God back into the city. If I find favor in the eyes of the LORD, he will bring me back and let me see both it and his dwelling place. But if he says, 'I have no pleasure in you,' behold, here I am, let him do to me what seems good to him." The king also said to Zadok the priest, "Are you not a seer? Go back to the city in peace, with your two sons, Ahimaaz your son, and Jonathan the son of Abiathar. See, I will wait at the fords of the wilderness until word comes from you to inform me." So Zadok and Abiathar carried the ark of God back to Jerusalem, and they remained there.

But David went up the ascent of the Mount of Olives, weeping as he went, barefoot and with his head covered. And all the people who were with him covered their heads, and they went up, weeping as they went. And it was told David, "Ahithophel is among the conspirators with Absalom." And David said, "O LORD, please turn the counsel of Ahithophel into foolishness."

While David was coming to the summit, where God was worshiped, behold, Hushai the Archite came to meet him with his coat torn and dirt on his head. David said to him, "If you go on with me, you will be a burden to me. But if you return to the city and say to Absalom, 'I will be your servant, O king; as I have been your father's servant in time past, so now I will be your servant,' then you will defeat for me the counsel of Ahithophel. Are not Zadok and Abiathar the priests with you there? So whatever you hear from the king's house, tell it to Zadok and Abiathar the priests. Behold, their two sons are with them there, Ahimaaz, Zadok's son, and Jonathan, Abiathar's son, and by them you shall send to me everything you hear." So Hushai, David's friend, came into the city, just as Absalom was entering Jerusalem.

1. *How gullible are the Israelites to believe Absalom's promises? Do we tend to believe the promises of politicians, particularly when they are not in power? Why? Do we want something for nothing?*

2. *Loyalty is tested whenever we lose position, power, or wealth. How loyal are we to friends who fail? Do we jump on the bandwagon of winners?*

3. *Why does David do nothing to stop Absalom at this time?*

DAY FOUR READING AND QUESTIONS

When David had passed a little beyond the summit, Ziba the servant of Mephibosheth met him, with a couple of donkeys saddled, bearing two hundred loaves of bread, a hundred bunches of raisins, a hundred of summer fruits, and a skin of wine. And the king said to Ziba, "Why have you brought these?" Ziba answered, "The donkeys are for the king's household to ride on, the bread and summer fruit for the young men to eat, and the wine for those who faint in the wilderness to drink." And the king said, "And where is your master's son?" Ziba said to the king, "Behold, he remains in Jerusalem, for he said, 'Today the house of Israel will give me back the kingdom of my father.'" Then the king said to Ziba, "Behold, all that belonged to Mephibosheth is now yours." And Ziba said, "I pay homage; let me ever find favor in your sight, my lord the king."

When King David came to Bahurim, there came out a man of the family of the house of Saul, whose name was Shimei, the son of Gera, and as he came he cursed continually. And he threw stones at David and at all the servants of King David, and all the people and all the mighty men were on his right hand and on his left. And Shimei said as he cursed, "Get out, get out, you man of blood, you worthless man! The LORD has avenged on you all the blood of the house of Saul, in whose place you have reigned, and the LORD has given the kingdom into the hand of your son Absalom. See, your evil is on you, for you are a man of blood."

Then Abishai the son of Zeruiah said to the king, "Why should this dead dog curse my lord the king? Let me go over and take off his head." But the king said, "What have I to do with you, you sons of Zeruiah? If he is cursing because the LORD has said to him, 'Curse David,' who then shall say, 'Why have you done so?'" And David said to Abishai and to all his servants, "Behold, my own son seeks my life; how much more now may this Benjaminite! Leave him alone, and let him curse, for the LORD has told him to. It may be that the LORD will look on the wrong done to me, and that the LORD will repay me with good for his cursing today." So David and his men went on the road, while Shimei went along on the hillside opposite him and cursed as he went and threw stones at him and flung dust. And the king, and all the people who were with him, arrived weary at the Jordan. And there he refreshed himself.

1. *If Mephibosheth is guilty of turning against David, how amazing is his ingratitude?*

2. *Why does David have no friends he can fully trust? How far can we trust our friends? How far can they trust us?*

3. *Do others ever criticize us unfairly? How do we react? Even if others lie about us, are they not making up for criticism we know we do deserve?*

DAY FIVE READING AND QUESTIONS

Go back and read 2 Samuel 13:1–16:14.

1. *Although we are not completely responsible for the actions of our children (we believe they have free will), don't they usually live out what we have taught them at home? Why do so many righteous people—Eli, Samuel, David—have children who turn against God? How could David have prevented Absalom's rebellion? How can we prevent our children from rebelling?*

2. *God had promised David the kingdom, but here he (at least temporarily) loses it. Do God's promises to us come true immediately? What should we do when we do not have what God has promised (see Heb. 11:13, 39)?*

3. *How do the events of these chapters show that God is disciplining David?*

Meditation on 2 Samuel 13:1–16:14

At times, the Word of the Lord is not an easy word to hear, particularly when it is a word of judgment. God has forgiven David, but he has also pronounced a word of punishment: "The sword will never depart from your house" (2 Sam. 12:10 NIV). In this section, David's children commit rape, murder, deceit, and rebellion. David is reaping what he has sown.

Absalom plays the politician running for office, working hard to get public opinion on his side. He causes a stir wherever he goes, riding in a chariot with fifty soldiers accompanying him. He listens closely to people's complaints, sympathizing with them and promising justice. If only he were king! He kisses everyone, not just babies.

After four years of this strategy, Absalom thinks he is strong enough to capture the throne. Asking permission of David to go to Hebron, Absalom sends messengers throughout Israel to proclaim him as king. David and his entire court must flee Jerusalem in fear for their lives.

As David and his supporters journey in exile, Shimei, a relative of Saul, comes out to curse them and throw stones at them. Shimei says the Lord has condemned David for his bloody murder of Saul's family. We, however, know Shimei is wrong. David showed great restraint in not killing Saul; he lamented the death of Saul and his sons; and he showed great mercy to Mephibosheth, grandson of Saul. David's guards want to shut up Shimei by cutting off his head.

However, David says to let him alone. Perhaps the Lord is telling Shimei to curse David. This does not mean David believes he is guilty of vengeance toward Saul's family, but it does reflect his acceptance of God's righteous punishment of his sin regarding Uriah and Bathsheba.

Yet the Lord has not abandoned David.

"God of grace, like David, may we accept your punishment as discipline to bring us closer to you."

A GOD WHO RESTORES

16:15–20:26 ESV

DAY ONE READING AND QUESTIONS

Now Absalom and all the people, the men of Israel, came to Jerusalem, and Ahithophel with him. And when Hushai the Archite, David's friend, came to Absalom, Hushai said to Absalom, "Long live the king! Long live the king!" And Absalom said to Hushai, "Is this your loyalty to your friend? Why did you not go with your friend?" And Hushai said to Absalom, "No, for whom the LORD and this people and all the men of Israel have chosen, his I will be, and with him I will remain. And again, whom should I serve? Should it not be his son? As I have served your father, so I will serve you."

Then Absalom said to Ahithophel, "Give your counsel. What shall we do?" Ahithophel said to Absalom, "Go in to your father's concubines, whom he has left to keep the house, and all Israel will hear that you have made yourself a stench to your father, and the hands of all who are with you will be strengthened." So they pitched a tent for Absalom on the roof. And Absalom went in to his father's concubines in the sight of all Israel. Now in those days the counsel that Ahithophel gave was as if one consulted the word of God; so was all the counsel of Ahithophel esteemed, both by David and by Absalom.

Moreover, Ahithophel said to Absalom, "Let me choose twelve thousand men, and I will arise and pursue David tonight. I will come upon him while he is weary and discouraged and throw him into a panic, and all the people who are with him will flee. I will strike down only the king, and I will bring all the people back to you as a bride comes home to her husband. You seek the life of only one man, and all the people will be at peace." And the advice seemed right in the eyes of Absalom and all the elders of Israel.

Then Absalom said, "Call Hushai the Archite also, and let us hear what he has to say." And when Hushai came to Absalom, Absalom said to him, "Thus has Ahithophel spoken; shall we do as he says? If not, you speak." Then Hushai said to Absalom, "This time the counsel that Ahithophel has given is not good." Hushai said, "You know that your father and his men are mighty men, and that they are enraged, like a bear robbed of her cubs in the field. Besides, your father is expert in war; he will not spend the night with the people. Behold, even now he has hidden himself in one of the pits or in some other place. And as soon as some of the people fall at the first attack, whoever hears it will say, 'There has been a slaughter among the people who follow Absalom.' Then even the valiant man, whose heart is like the heart of a lion, will utterly melt with fear, for all Israel knows that your father is a mighty man, and that those who are with him are valiant men. But my counsel is that all Israel be gathered to you, from Dan to Beersheba, as the sand by the sea for multitude, and that you go to battle in person. So we shall come upon him in some place where he is to be found, and we shall light upon him as the dew falls on the ground, and of him and all the men with him not one will be left. If he withdraws into a city, then all Israel will bring ropes to that city, and we shall drag it into the valley, until not even a pebble is to be found there." And Absalom and all the men of Israel said, "The counsel of Hushai the Archite is better than the counsel of Ahithophel." For the LORD had ordained to defeat the good counsel of Ahithophel, so that the LORD might bring harm upon Absalom.

Then Hushai said to Zadok and Abiathar the priests, "Thus and so did Ahithophel counsel Absalom and the elders of

Israel, and thus and so have I counseled. Now therefore send quickly and tell David, 'Do not stay tonight at the fords of the wilderness, but by all means pass over, lest the king and all the people who are with him be swallowed up.'" Now Jonathan and Ahimaaz were waiting at En-rogel. A female servant was to go and tell them, and they were to go and tell King David, for they were not to be seen entering the city. But a young man saw them and told Absalom. So both of them went away quickly and came to the house of a man at Bahurim, who had a well in his courtyard. And they went down into it. And the woman took and spread a covering over the well's mouth and scattered grain on it, and nothing was known of it. When Absalom's servants came to the woman at the house, they said, "Where are Ahimaaz and Jonathan?" And the woman said to them, "They have gone over the brook of water." And when they had sought and could not find them, they returned to Jerusalem.

After they had gone, the men came up out of the well, and went and told King David. They said to David, "Arise, and go quickly over the water, for thus and so has Ahithophel counseled against you." Then David arose, and all the people who were with him, and they crossed the Jordan. By daybreak not one was left who had not crossed the Jordan.

When Ahithophel saw that his counsel was not followed, he saddled his donkey and went off home to his own city. He set his house in order and hanged himself, and he died and was buried in the tomb of his father.

Then David came to Mahanaim. And Absalom crossed the Jordan with all the men of Israel. Now Absalom had set Amasa over the army instead of Joab. Amasa was the son of a man named Ithra the Ishmaelite, who had married Abigal the daughter of Nahash, sister of Zeruiah, Joab's mother. And Israel and Absalom encamped in the land of Gilead.

When David came to Mahanaim, Shobi the son of Nahash from Rabbah of the Ammonites, and Machir the son of Ammiel from Lo-debar, and Barzillai the Gileadite from Rogelim, brought beds, basins, and earthen vessels, wheat, barley, flour, parched grain, beans and lentils, honey and curds and sheep and cheese from the herd, for David and the people with him to eat, for they said, "The people are hungry and weary and thirsty in the wilderness."

1. *Absalom considered Ahithophel's advice as sure as the voice of God (2 Sam. 16:23). Why then did Absalom not listen to Ahithophel?*

2. *Who are your wisest advisors? Do you listen to them? What is the true source of all wisdom (see James 1:5)?*

3. *Why did Ahithophel take his own life? What drove him to such despair? Did he have a healthy view of his own worth? Do we?*

DAY TWO READING AND QUESTIONS

Then David mustered the men who were with him and set over them commanders of thousands and commanders of hundreds. And David sent out the army, one third under the command of Joab, one third under the command of Abishai the son of Zeruiah, Joab's brother, and one third under the command of Ittai the Gittite. And the king said to the men, "I myself will also go out with you." But the men said, "You shall not go out. For if we flee, they will not care about us. If half of us die, they will not care about us. But you are worth ten thousand of us. Therefore it is better that you send us help from the city." The king said to them, "Whatever seems best to you I will do." So the king stood at the side of the gate, while all the army marched out by hundreds and by thousands. And the king ordered Joab and Abishai and Ittai, "Deal gently for my sake with the young man Absalom." And all the people heard when the king gave orders to all the commanders about Absalom.

So the army went out into the field against Israel, and the battle was fought in the forest of Ephraim. And the men of Israel were defeated there by the servants of David, and the loss there was great on that day, twenty thousand men. The battle spread over the face of all the country, and the forest devoured more people that day than the sword.

And Absalom happened to meet the servants of David. Absalom was riding on his mule, and the mule went under the thick branches of a great oak, and his head caught fast in the oak, and he was suspended between heaven and earth, while the mule that was under him went on. And a certain man saw it and told Joab, "Behold, I saw Absalom hanging in an oak." Joab said to the man who told him, "What, you saw him! Why then did you not strike him there to the ground? I would have been glad to give you ten pieces of silver and a belt." But the man said to Joab, "Even if I felt in my hand the weight of a thousand pieces of silver, I would not reach out my hand against the king's son, for in our hearing the king commanded you and Abishai and Ittai, 'For my sake protect the young man Absalom.' On the other hand, if I had dealt treacherously against his life (and there is nothing hidden from the king), then you yourself would have stood aloof." Joab said, "I will not waste time like this with you." And he took three javelins in his hand and thrust them into the heart of Absalom while he was still alive in the oak. And ten young men, Joab's armor-bearers, surrounded Absalom and struck him and killed him.

Then Joab blew the trumpet, and the troops came back from pursuing Israel, for Joab restrained them. And they took Absalom and threw him into a great pit in the forest and raised over him a very great heap of stones. And all Israel fled every one to his own home. Now Absalom in his lifetime had taken and set up for himself the pillar that is in the King's Valley, for he said, "I have no son to keep my name in remembrance." He called the pillar after his own name, and it is called Absalom's monument to this day.

Then Ahimaaz the son of Zadok said, "Let me run and carry news to the king that the LORD has delivered him from the hand of his enemies." And Joab said to him, "You are not to carry news today. You may carry news another day, but today you shall carry no news, because the king's son is dead." Then Joab said to the Cushite, "Go, tell the king what you have seen." The Cushite bowed before Joab, and ran. Then Ahimaaz the son of Zadok said again to Joab, "Come what may, let me also run after the Cushite." And Joab said, "Why will you run, my son, seeing that you will have no reward for the news?" "Come what may," he said, "I will run." So he said to him, "Run." Then Ahimaaz ran by the way of the plain, and outran the Cushite.

Now David was sitting between the two gates, and the watchman went up to the roof of the gate by the wall, and when he lifted up his eyes and looked, he saw a man running alone. The watchman called out and told the king. And the king said, "If he is alone, there is news in his mouth." And he drew nearer and nearer. The watchman saw another man running. And the watchman called to the gate and said, "See, another man running alone!" The king said, "He also brings news." The watchman said, "I think the running of the first is like the running of Ahimaaz the son of Zadok." And the king said, "He is a good man and comes with good news."

Then Ahimaaz cried out to the king, "All is well." And he bowed before the king with his face to the earth and said, "Blessed be the LORD your God, who has delivered up the men who raised their hand against my lord the king." And the king said, "Is it well with the young man Absalom?" Ahimaaz answered, "When Joab sent the king's servant, your servant, I saw a great commotion, but I do not know what it was." And the king said, "Turn aside and stand here." So he turned aside and stood still.

And behold, the Cushite came, and the Cushite said, "Good news for my lord the king! For the LORD has delivered you this day from the hand of all who rose up against you." The king said to the Cushite, "Is it well with the young man Absalom?" And the Cushite answered, "May the enemies of my lord the king and all who rise up against you for evil be like that young man." And the king was deeply moved and went up to the chamber over the gate and wept. And as he went, he said, "O my son Absalom, my son, my son Absalom! Would I had died instead of you, O Absalom, my son, my son!"

It was told Joab, "Behold, the king is weeping and mourning for Absalom." So the victory that day was turned into mourning for all the people, for the people heard that day, "The king is grieving for his son." And the people stole into the city that day as people steal in who are ashamed when they flee in battle. The king covered his face, and the king cried with a loud voice, "O my son Absalom, O Absalom, my son, my son!" Then Joab came into the house to the king and said, "You have today covered with shame the faces of all your servants, who have this day saved your life and the lives of your sons and your daughters and the lives of your wives and your concubines, because you love those who hate you and hate those who love you. For you have made it clear today that commanders and servants are nothing to you, for today I know that if Absalom were alive and all of us were dead today, then you would be pleased. Now therefore arise, go out and speak kindly to your servants, for I swear by the LORD, if you do not go, not a man will stay with you this night, and this will be worse for you than all the evil that has come upon you from your youth until now." Then the king arose and took his seat in the gate. And the people were all told, "Behold, the king is sitting in the gate." And all the people came before the king.

1. *Is Joab right to kill Absalom, against the direct orders of David? Why does he kill him? Who is more concerned with the kingdom of Israel in this story, Joab or David?*

2. *Could you under any circumstances order the death of your child? What if that child were a convicted murderer? A terrorist? How did Abraham feel about offering his son (Gen. 22)?*

3. *If we cannot easily offer our children to death, even if they deserve it, then how much does God love us (John 3:16)?*

DAY THREE READING AND QUESTIONS

Now Israel had fled every man to his own home. And all the people were arguing throughout all the tribes of Israel, saying, "The king delivered us from the hand of our enemies and saved us from the hand of the Philistines, and now he has fled out of the land from Absalom. But Absalom, whom we anointed over us, is dead in battle. Now therefore why do you say nothing about bringing the king back?"

And King David sent this message to Zadok and Abiathar the priests: "Say to the elders of Judah, 'Why should you be the last to bring the king back to his house, when the word of all Israel has come to the king? You are my brothers; you are my bone and my flesh. Why then should you be the last to bring back the king?' And say to Amasa, 'Are you not my bone and my flesh? God do so to me and more also, if you are not commander of my army from now on in place of Joab.'" And he swayed the heart of all the men of Judah as one man, so that they sent word to the king, "Return, both you and all your servants." So the king came back to the Jordan, and Judah came to Gilgal to meet the king and to bring the king over the Jordan.

And Shimei the son of Gera, the Benjaminite, from Bahurim, hurried to come down with the men of Judah to meet King David. And with him were a thousand men from Benjamin. And Ziba the servant of the house of Saul, with his fifteen sons and his twenty servants, rushed down to the Jordan before the king, and they crossed the ford to bring over the king's household and to do his pleasure. And Shimei the son of Gera fell down before the king, as he was about to cross the Jordan, and said to the king, "Let not my lord hold me guilty or remember how your servant did wrong on the day my lord the king left Jerusalem. Do not let the king take it to heart. For your servant knows that I have sinned. Therefore, behold, I have come this day, the first of all the house of Joseph to come down to meet my lord the king." Abishai the son of Zeruiah answered, "Shall not Shimei be put to death for this, because he cursed the LORD's anointed?" But David said, "What have I to do with you, you sons of Zeruiah, that you should this day be as an adversary to me? Shall anyone be put to death in Israel this day? For do I not know that I am this day king over Israel?" And the king said to Shimei, "You shall not die." And the king gave him his oath.

And Mephibosheth the son of Saul came down to meet the king. He had neither taken care of his feet nor trimmed his beard nor washed his clothes, from the day the king departed until the day he came back in safety. And when he came to Jerusalem to meet the king, the king said to him, "Why did you not go with me, Mephibosheth?" He answered, "My lord, O king, my servant deceived me, for your servant said to him, 'I will saddle a donkey for myself, that I may ride on it and go with the king.' For your servant is lame. He has slandered your servant to my lord the king. But my lord the king is like the angel of God; do therefore what seems good to you. For all my father's house were but men doomed to death before my lord the king, but you set your servant among those who eat at your table. What further right have I, then, to cry to the king?" And the king said to him, "Why speak any more of your affairs? I have decided: you and Ziba shall divide the land." And Mephibosheth said to the king, "Oh, let him take it all, since my lord the king has come safely home."

Now Barzillai the Gileadite had come down from Rogelim, and he went on with the king to the Jordan, to escort him over the Jordan. Barzillai was a very aged man, eighty years old. He had provided the king with food while he stayed at Mahanaim, for he was a very wealthy man. And the king said to Barzillai, "Come over with me, and I will provide for you with me in Jerusalem." But Barzillai said to the king, "How many years have I still to live, that I should go up with the king to Jerusalem? I am this day eighty years old. Can I discern what is pleasant and what is not? Can your servant taste what he eats or what he drinks? Can I still listen to the voice of singing men and singing women? Why then should your servant be an added burden to my lord the king? Your servant will go a little way over the Jordan with the king. Why should the king repay me with such a reward? Please let your servant return, that I may die in my own city near the grave of my father and my mother. But here is your servant Chimham. Let him go over with my lord the king, and do for him whatever seems good to you." And the king answered, "Chimham shall go over with me, and I will do for him whatever seems good to you, and all that you desire of me I will do for you." Then all the people went over the Jordan, and the king went over. And the king kissed Barzillai and blessed him, and he returned to his own home. The king went on to Gilgal, and Chimham went on with him. All the people of Judah, and also half the people of Israel, brought the king on his way.

Then all the men of Israel came to the king and said to the king, "Why have our brothers the men of Judah stolen you away and brought the king and his household over the Jordan, and all David's men with him?" All the men of Judah answered the men of Israel, "Because the king is our close relative. Why then are you angry over this matter? Have we eaten at all at the king's expense? Or has he given us any gift?" And the men of Israel answered the men of Judah, "We have ten shares in the king, and in David also we have more than you. Why then did you despise us? Were we not the first to speak of bringing back our king?" But the words of the men of Judah were fiercer than the words of the men of Israel.

1. *Whose story do you believe, Ziba's or Mephibosheth's? Why?*

2. *How can you tell when someone is telling the truth? How can you tell someone is truly loyal?*

3. *Why does David forgive Shimei? Have you even had to forgive someone who stabbed you in the back? How hard was it?*

DAY FOUR READING AND QUESTIONS

Now there happened to be there a worthless man, whose name was Sheba, the son of Bichri, a Benjaminite. And he blew the trumpet and said,

> "We have no portion in David,
> and we have no inheritance in the son of Jesse;
> every man to his tents, O Israel!"

So all the men of Israel withdrew from David and followed Sheba the son of Bichri. But the men of Judah followed their king steadfastly from the Jordan to Jerusalem.

And David came to his house at Jerusalem. And the king took the ten concubines whom he had left to care for the house and put them in a house under guard and provided for them, but did not go in to them. So they were shut up until the day of their death, living as if in widowhood.

Then the king said to Amasa, "Call the men of Judah together to me within three days, and be here yourself." So Amasa went to summon Judah, but he delayed beyond the set time that had been appointed him. And David said to Abishai, "Now Sheba the son of Bichri will do us more harm than Absalom. Take your lord's servants and pursue him, lest he get himself to fortified cities and escape from us." And there went out after him Joab's men and the Cherethites and the Pelethites, and all the mighty men. They went out from Jerusalem to pursue Sheba the son of Bichri. When they were at the great stone that is in Gibeon, Amasa came to meet them. Now Joab was wearing a soldier's garment, and over it was a belt with a sword in its sheath fastened on his thigh, and as he went forward it fell out. And Joab said to Amasa, "Is it well with you, my brother?" And Joab took Amasa by the beard with his right hand to kiss him. But Amasa did not observe the sword that was in Joab's hand. So Joab struck him with it in the stomach and spilled his entrails to the ground without striking a second blow, and he died.

Then Joab and Abishai his brother pursued Sheba the son of Bichri. And one of Joab's young men took his stand by Amasa and said, "Whoever favors Joab, and whoever is for David, let him follow Joab." And Amasa lay wallowing in his blood in the highway. And anyone who came by, seeing him, stopped. And when the man saw that all the people stopped, he carried Amasa out of the highway into the field and threw a garment over him. When he was taken out of the highway, all the people went on after Joab to pursue Sheba the son of Bichri.

And Sheba passed through all the tribes of Israel to Abel of Beth-maacah, and all the Bichrites assembled and followed him in. And all the men who were with Joab came and besieged him in Abel of Beth-maacah. They cast up a mound against the city, and it stood against the rampart, and they were battering the wall to throw it down. Then a wise woman called from the city, "Listen! Listen! Tell Joab, 'Come here, that I may speak to you.'" And he came near her, and the woman said, "Are you Joab?" He answered, "I am." Then she said to him, "Listen to the words of your servant." And he answered, "I am listening." Then she said, "They used to say in former times, 'Let them but ask counsel at Abel,' and so they settled a matter. I am one of those who are peaceable and faithful in Israel. You seek to destroy a city that is a mother in Israel. Why will you swallow up the heritage of the Lord?" Joab answered, "Far be it from me, far be it, that I should swallow up or destroy! That is not true. But a man of the hill country of Ephraim, called Sheba the son of Bichri, has lifted up his hand against King David. Give up him alone, and I will withdraw from the city." And the woman said to Joab, "Behold, his head shall be thrown to you over the wall." Then the woman went to all the people in her wisdom. And they cut off the head of Sheba the son of Bichri and threw it out to Joab. So he blew the trumpet, and they dispersed from the city, every man to his home. And Joab returned to Jerusalem to the king.

Now Joab was in command of all the army of Israel; and Benaiah the son of Jehoiada was in command of the Cherethites and the Pelethites; and Adoram was in charge of the forced labor; and Jehoshaphat the son of Ahilud was the recorder; and Sheva was secretary; and Zadok and Abiathar were priests; and Ira the Jairite was also David's priest.

1. *Why was Sheba's rebellion so popular in Israel? Why did so many have trouble being loyal to David? What was God's hand in all this?*

2. *Contrast Joab's actions toward his enemies with David's. Whose policy is more effective? Whose is more godly?*

3. *How should we treat rivals?*

DAY FIVE READING AND QUESTIONS

Go back and read 2 Samuel 16:15–20:26.

1. *What lessons had David learned in exile? How do hard times sometimes teach us important lessons? What have you learned when friends have turned against you?*

2. *God restores David to the throne. How has God brought you out of bad times? When do we feel closer to God, when times are tough or when he obviously blesses us?*

3. *Will God always restore the fortunes of his people?*

Meditation on 2 Samuel 16:15–20:26

In this civil war, David intends to take to the field himself against Absalom's army, but his men will not let him take the risk. He therefore sends out his troops under three commanders, giving them instructions to be gentle with Absalom himself.

David's forces are victorious. Absalom rides his mule under a tree during the battle and gets his long hair stuck in the branches, and the mule runs on, leaving Absalom hanging from the tree. One of David's soldiers reports to Joab that he saw Absalom hanging helplessly in the tree. While the soldier refuses to kill Absalom for David's sake, Joab is not so reticent. He plunges three javelins into Absalom's heart, and his men finish the job, unceremoniously dumping his body in a pit.

David does not take the news as joyous victory over an enemy but as the loss of a beloved son. His grief is so great, he wishes he had died instead of Absalom. Such grief demoralizes his army. So much so that Joab warns David to show some appreciation for those who risked their lives for him; otherwise, all might desert. David then sits in the gate of the city to receive his returning soldiers.

If the Lord is a God who punishes sin, he is also a God who restores our fortunes when we turn back to him. Although the price of David's sins is high—death of his sons, cursing, and exile—God forgives him, brings him back to Jerusalem, and restores the kingdom to him. Even when we turn against God, his anger is not forever. If we again hear his voice, he will restore us.

"God of love, restore us to you!"

A GOD WHO MAKES COVENANT

21:1–17; 22:1–23:17; 24:1–25 ESV

DAY ONE READING AND QUESTIONS

Now there was a famine in the days of David for three years, year after year. And David sought the face of the LORD. And the LORD said, "There is bloodguilt on Saul and on his house, because he put the Gibeonites to death." So the king called the Gibeonites and spoke to them. Now the Gibeonites were not of the people of Israel but of the remnant of the Amorites. Although the people of Israel had sworn to spare them, Saul had sought to strike them down in his zeal for the people of Israel and Judah. And David said to the Gibeonites, "What shall I do for you? And how shall I make atonement, that you may bless the heritage of the LORD?" The Gibeonites said to him, "It is not a matter of silver or gold between us and Saul or his house; neither is it for us to put any man to death in Israel." And he said, "What do you say that I shall do for you?" They said to the king, "The man who consumed us and planned to destroy us, so that we should have no place in all the territory of Israel, let seven of his sons be given to us, so that we may hang them before the LORD at Gibeah of Saul, the chosen of the LORD." And the king said, "I will give them."

But the king spared Mephibosheth, the son of Saul's son Jonathan, because of the oath of the LORD that was between them, between David and Jonathan the son of Saul. The king took the two sons of Rizpah the daughter of Aiah, whom she bore to Saul, Armoni and Mephibosheth; and the five sons of Merab the daughter of Saul, whom she bore to Adriel the son of Barzillai the Meholathite; and he gave them into the hands of the Gibeonites, and they hanged them on the mountain before the LORD, and the seven of them perished together. They were put to death in the first days of harvest, at the beginning of barley harvest.

Then Rizpah the daughter of Aiah took sackcloth and spread it for herself on the rock, from the beginning of harvest until rain fell upon them from the heavens. And she did not allow the birds of the air to come upon them by day, or the beasts of the field by night. When David was told what Rizpah the daughter of Aiah, the concubine of Saul, had done, David went and took the bones of Saul and the bones of his son Jonathan from the men of Jabesh-gilead, who had stolen them from the public square of Beth-shan, where the Philistines had hanged them, on the day the Philistines killed Saul on Gilboa. And he brought up from there the bones of Saul and the bones of his son Jonathan; and they gathered the bones of those who were hanged. And they buried the bones of Saul and his son Jonathan in the land of Benjamin in Zela, in the tomb of Kish his father. And they did all that the king commanded. And after that God responded to the plea for the land.

There was war again between the Philistines and Israel, and David went down together with his servants, and they fought against the Philistines. And David grew weary. And Ishbi-benob, one of the descendants of the giants, whose spear weighed three hundred shekels of bronze, and who was armed with a new sword, thought to kill David. But Abishai the son of Zeruiah came to his aid and attacked the Philistine and killed him. Then David's men swore to him, "You shall no longer go out with us to battle, lest you quench the lamp of Israel."

1. *Is God just to punish Israel for the sins of Saul long after his death?*

2. *Do the consequences of sin affect later generations? How have you been affected by the sins of your parents and grandparents?*

3. *How should we show loyalty to the dead? What are some of our funeral customs that show respect? Are such customs morbid or helpful?*

DAY TWO READING AND QUESTIONS

And David spoke to the LORD the words of this song on the day when the LORD delivered him from the hand of all his enemies, and from the hand of Saul. He said,

> "The LORD is my rock and my fortress and my deliverer,
> my God, my rock, in whom I take refuge,
> my shield, and the horn of my salvation,
> my stronghold and my refuge,
> my savior; you save me from violence.
> I call upon the LORD, who is worthy to be praised,
> and I am saved from my enemies.
>
> "For the waves of death encompassed me,
> the torrents of destruction assailed me;
> the cords of Sheol entangled me;
> the snares of death confronted me.
>
> "In my distress I called upon the LORD;
> to my God I called.
> From his temple he heard my voice,
> and my cry came to his ears.
>
> "Then the earth reeled and rocked;
> the foundations of the heavens trembled

and quaked, because he was angry.
Smoke went up from his nostrils,
and devouring fire from his mouth;
glowing coals flamed forth from him.
He bowed the heavens and came down;
thick darkness was under his feet.
He rode on a cherub and flew;
he was seen on the wings of the wind.
He made darkness around him his canopy,
thick clouds, a gathering of water.
Out of the brightness before him
coals of fire flamed forth.
The LORD thundered from heaven,
and the Most High uttered his voice.
And he sent out arrows and scattered them;
lightning, and routed them.
Then the channels of the sea were seen;
the foundations of the world were laid bare,
at the rebuke of the LORD,
at the blast of the breath of his nostrils.

"He sent from on high, he took me;
he drew me out of many waters.
He rescued me from my strong enemy,
from those who hated me,
for they were too mighty for me.
They confronted me in the day of my calamity,
but the LORD was my support.
He brought me out into a broad place;
he rescued me, because he delighted in me.

"The LORD dealt with me according to my righteousness;
according to the cleanness of my hands he rewarded me.
For I have kept the ways of the LORD

and have not wickedly departed from my God.
For all his rules were before me,
and from his statutes I did not turn aside.
I was blameless before him,
and I kept myself from guilt.
And the LORD has rewarded me according to my righteousness,
according to my cleanness in his sight.

"With the merciful you show yourself merciful;
with the blameless man you show yourself blameless;
with the purified you deal purely,
and with the crooked you make yourself seem tortuous.
You save a humble people,
but your eyes are on the haughty to bring them down.
For you are my lamp, O LORD,
and my God lightens my darkness.
For by you I can run against a troop,
and by my God I can leap over a wall.
This God—his way is perfect;
the word of the LORD proves true;
he is a shield for all those who take refuge in him.

"For who is God, but the LORD?
And who is a rock, except our God?
This God is my strong refuge
and has made my way blameless.
He made my feet like the feet of a deer
and set me secure on the heights.
He trains my hands for war,
so that my arms can bend a bow of bronze.
You have given me the shield of your salvation,
and your gentleness made me great.
You gave a wide place for my steps under me,

and my feet did not slip;
I pursued my enemies and destroyed them,
and did not turn back until they were consumed.
I consumed them; I thrust them through, so that they did not rise;
they fell under my feet.
For you equipped me with strength for the battle;
you made those who rise against me sink under me.
You made my enemies turn their backs to me,
those who hated me, and I destroyed them.
They looked, but there was none to save;
they cried to the LORD, but he did not answer them.
I beat them fine as the dust of the earth;
I crushed them and stamped them down like the mire of the streets.

"You delivered me from strife with my people;
you kept me as the head of the nations;
people whom I had not known served me.
Foreigners came cringing to me;
as soon as they heard of me, they obeyed me.
Foreigners lost heart
and came trembling out of their fortresses.

"The LORD lives, and blessed be my rock,
and exalted be my God, the rock of my salvation,
the God who gave me vengeance
and brought down peoples under me,
who brought me out from my enemies;
you exalted me above those who rose against me;
you delivered me from men of violence.

"For this I will praise you, O LORD, among the nations,
and sing praises to your name.

Great salvation he brings to his king,
and shows steadfast love to his anointed,
to David and his offspring forever."

1. *Compare this song to some of the songs we sing in worship. For what do we praise God?*

2. *Are our songs primarily about our feelings or about God's actions? What can we learn about praising God from this song?*

3. *In what circumstances has God been your rock? Has he saved you from death? From what enemies has he delivered you?*

DAY THREE READING AND QUESTIONS

Now these are the last words of David:

The oracle of David, the son of Jesse,
the oracle of the man who was raised on high,
the anointed of the God of Jacob,
the sweet psalmist of Israel:

"The Spirit of the Lord speaks by me;
his word is on my tongue.
The God of Israel has spoken;
the Rock of Israel has said to me:
When one rules justly over men,
ruling in the fear of God,
he dawns on them like the morning light,
like the sun shining forth on a cloudless morning,
like rain that makes grass to sprout from the earth.

"For does not my house stand so with God?
For he has made with me an everlasting covenant,
ordered in all things and secure.
For will he not cause to prosper
all my help and my desire?
But worthless men are all like thorns that are thrown away,
for they cannot be taken with the hand;
but the man who touches them
arms himself with iron and the shaft of a spear,
and they are utterly consumed with fire."

These are the names of the mighty men whom David had: Josheb-basshebeth a Tahchemonite; he was chief of the three. He wielded his spear against eight hundred whom he killed at one time.

And next to him among the three mighty men was Eleazar the son of Dodo, son of Ahohi. He was with David when they defied the Philistines who were gathered there for battle, and the men of Israel withdrew. He rose and struck down the Philistines until his hand was weary, and his hand clung to the sword. And the LORD brought about a great victory that day, and the men returned after him only to strip the slain.

And next to him was Shammah, the son of Agee the Hararite. The Philistines gathered together at Lehi, where there was a plot of ground full of lentils, and the men fled from the Philistines. But he took his stand in the midst of the plot and defended it and struck down the Philistines, and the LORD worked a great victory.

And three of the thirty chief men went down and came about harvest time to David at the cave of Adullam, when a band of Philistines was encamped in the Valley of Rephaim. David was then in the stronghold, and the garrison of the Philistines was then at Bethlehem. And David said longingly,

> "Oh, that someone would give me water to drink from the well of Bethlehem that is by the gate!" Then the three mighty men broke through the camp of the Philistines and drew water out of the well of Bethlehem that was by the gate and carried and brought it to David. But he would not drink of it. He poured it out to the LORD and said, "Far be it from me, O LORD, that I should do this. Shall I drink the blood of the men who went at the risk of their lives?" Therefore he would not drink it. These things the three mighty men did.

1. *Is there a place for boasting of our relationship with God? What about Paul in 2 Corinthians 11:16–33? When is boasting bad?*

2. *Why did the mighty men get water for David? Why would David pour out water that almost cost his men their lives? How do you think the men felt about it? What is a gift you received that you felt was too good for you?*

3. *Why do you think David's mighty warriors are listed here?*

DAY FOUR READING AND QUESTIONS

> Again the anger of the LORD was kindled against Israel, and he incited David against them, saying, "Go, number Israel and Judah." So the king said to Joab, the commander of the army, who was with him, "Go through all the tribes of Israel, from Dan to Beersheba, and number the people, that I may know the number of the people." But Joab said to the king, "May the LORD your God add to the people a hundred times as many as

they are, while the eyes of my lord the king still see it, but why does my lord the king delight in this thing?" But the king's word prevailed against Joab and the commanders of the army. So Joab and the commanders of the army went out from the presence of the king to number the people of Israel. They crossed the Jordan and began from Aroer, and from the city that is in the middle of the valley, toward Gad and on to Jazer. Then they came to Gilead, and to Kadesh in the land of the Hittites; and they came to Dan, and from Dan they went around to Sidon, and came to the fortress of Tyre and to all the cities of the Hivites and Canaanites; and they went out to the Negeb of Judah at Beersheba. So when they had gone through all the land, they came to Jerusalem at the end of nine months and twenty days. And Joab gave the sum of the numbering of the people to the king: in Israel there were 800,000 valiant men who drew the sword, and the men of Judah were 500,000.

But David's heart struck him after he had numbered the people. And David said to the LORD, "I have sinned greatly in what I have done. But now, O LORD, please take away the iniquity of your servant, for I have done very foolishly." And when David arose in the morning, the word of the LORD came to the prophet Gad, David's seer, saying, "Go and say to David, 'Thus says the LORD, Three things I offer you. Choose one of them, that I may do it to you.'" So Gad came to David and told him, and said to him, "Shall three years of famine come to you in your land? Or will you flee three months before your foes while they pursue you? Or shall there be three days' pestilence in your land? Now consider, and decide what answer I shall return to him who sent me." Then David said to Gad, "I am in great distress. Let us fall into the hand of the LORD, for his mercy is great; but let me not fall into the hand of man."

So the LORD sent a pestilence on Israel from the morning until the appointed time. And there died of the people from Dan to Beersheba 70,000 men. And when the angel stretched out his hand toward Jerusalem to destroy it, the LORD relented from the calamity and said to the angel who was working destruction among the people, "It is enough; now stay your hand." And the angel of the LORD was by the threshing floor of Araunah the Jebusite. Then David spoke to the LORD when he saw the angel who was striking the people, and said, "Behold, I have sinned, and I have done wickedly. But these sheep, what have they done? Please let your hand be against me and against my father's house."

And Gad came that day to David and said to him, "Go up, raise an altar to the LORD on the threshing floor of Araunah the Jebusite." So David went up at Gad's word, as the LORD commanded. And when Araunah looked down, he saw the king and his servants coming on toward him. And Araunah went out and paid homage to the king with his face to the ground. And Araunah said, "Why has my lord the king come to his servant?" David said, "To buy the threshing floor from you, in order to build an altar to the LORD, that the plague may be averted from the people." Then Araunah said to David, "Let my lord the king take and offer up what seems good to him. Here are the oxen for the burnt offering and the threshing sledges and the yokes of the oxen for the wood. All this, O king, Araunah gives to the king." And Araunah said to the king, "May the LORD your God accept you." But the king said to Araunah, "No, but I will buy it from you for a price. I will not offer burnt offerings to the LORD my God that cost me nothing." So David bought the threshing floor and the oxen for fifty shekels of silver. And David built there an altar to the LORD and offered burnt offerings and peace offerings. So the LORD responded to the plea for the land, and the plague was averted from Israel.

1. *Why is the census a sin?*

2. *Should we be concerned with numbers as Christians? Should we count church attendance? Contributions? Are big churches more powerful than small ones? More influential? More faithful? Does God need big numbers to work his will?*

3. *Did David make the right choice of punishment? Should he not have taken more on himself? Which would you have chosen and why?*

DAY FIVE READING AND QUESTIONS

Go back and read 2 Samuel 21:1–17; 22:1–23:17; 24:1–25.

1. *Why does God punish Israel so often? What does God's punishment tell us about the importance of listening to him? Is punishment a sign of God's love? How?*

2. *David commits serious sins that have severe consequences. However, when confronted, he always turns back to God and accepts his discipline. Can we be confident of our relationship with God even when we sin?*

3. *Can we accept God's forgiveness like David? Can we forgive ourselves? Does sin always break our covenant with God?*

Meditation on 2 Samuel 21:1–17; 22:1–23:17; 24:1–25

David writes a great hymn of praise, also found in slightly different form in Psalm 18, calling God his rock and fortress, an apt metaphor in light of the many times the Lord has saved him from violent men. Indeed, the Lord has snatched him from the clutches of death itself.

The psalm continues by describing the Lord's power, thundering against his enemies. By contrast, the Lord has rewarded David for his steadfast righteousness, showing faithfulness to the faithful. The song ends with praise for all God has done for David, giving him victories, establishing his kingdom, and showing him unfailing kindness.

In his "last words," David rejoices that God has spoken through him. In what may seem like boasting, David sees himself as a righteous king, like the light of the morning. But he is not bragging on himself, but rather on the Lord who made covenant with him. David also honors the mighty men whom the Lord has used to bless Israel.

The books of Samuel end with another sin of David, one that is as severe in its consequences as his sin with Bathsheba. David decides to have a census and number his fighting men. The Lord sends the prophet Gad to David with three choices of punishment: three years of famine, three months of war, or three days of plague. Trusting the Lord's mercy, David chooses plague directly from God instead of punishment through men. Seventy thousand Israelites die in the plague, and just as the angel of death gets ready to strike Jerusalem, the Lord stays his hand.

The angel had stopped at the threshing floor of Araunah. David buys the threshing floor, erects an altar there, and offers sacrifices to God to stop the plague. God hears his prayer. This later would be the site of the temple built by Solomon (2 Chron. 3:1).

Thus the books of Samuel end as they began. As God heard the prayer of Hannah for a child, so he hears the prayer of David for forgiveness and deliverance. We serve a God who listens. We serve a God who speaks. The question Samuel raises for his original readers and for us is this: Will we listen to the voice of God?

"God who speaks, give us ears to hear and hearts to obey."

Ten Volumes Covering the Old Testament

Psalms
by Gary Holloway
ISBN 978-1-68426-261-8

Proverbs, Ecclesiastes, and Job
by Gary Holloway
ISBN 978-1-68426-432-2

Isaiah
by Gary Holloway
ISBN 978-1-68426-438-4

Jeremiah, Lamentations, Ezekiel, Daniel
by Gary Holloway
ISBN 978-1-68426-439-1

Hosea to Malachi
by Gary Holloway
ISBN 978-1-68426-440-7

www.leafwoodpublishers.com

Twelve Volumes Covering the New Testament

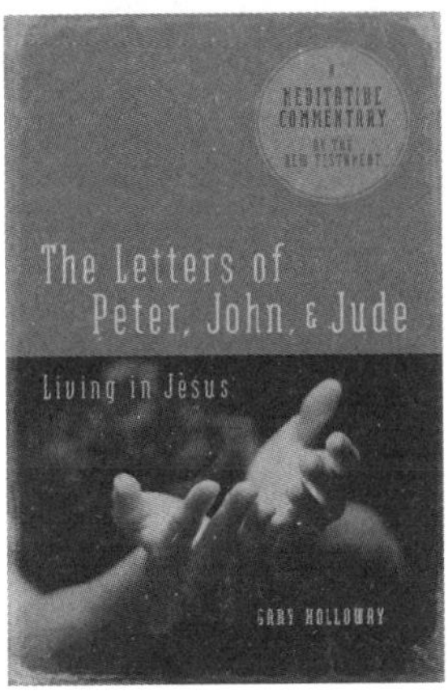

Ephesians, Philippians, Colossians, & Philemon
by Earl Lavender
ISBN 978-0-89112-561-7

1 & 2 Thessalonians, 1 & 2 Timothy, Titus
by Gary Holloway
ISBN 978-0-89112-503-7

Hebrews & James
by Gary Holloway
ISBN 978-0-89112-505-1

The Letters of Peter, John, & Jude
by Gary Holloway
ISBN 978-0-89112-557-0

Revelation
by Terry Briley
ISBN 978-0-89112-559-4

Do you want a deeper, more fulfilling way of Bible study? Do you want to know God through Scripture—not just to know the teachings but to have a relationship with the Teacher? This meditative commentary is for you. There are many commentaries on the books of the Bible, but this series is different. It employs the classic Christian method of "holy reading" to help you hear the voice of God.

Holy reading involves slowly engaging a short passage of Scripture, listening closely, reading repeatedly, praying the words, and perhaps sharing with fellow believers. God will bless us, our families, and our churches if we take the time to be still, listen, and do his word.

www.leafwoodpublishers.com